MW01504433

TRAVEL GUIDE

2024

The essential information you need to know before visting Kyoto. Tips and tricks for a seamless sojourn

JUDY HARRIS

TABLE OF CONTENTS

Important Notice Before You Continue Reading

Step into a world beyond your imagination. This extraordinary travel guide invites you to embark on a remarkable journey through Kyoto. Brace yourself for a truly immersive experience, where your imagination, creativity, and sense of adventure will be your compass. Leave behind the glossy images and preconceived notions because we believe that genuine beauty should be encountered firsthand, untainted by visual filters. Prepare yourself for an exhilarating exploration where every monument, every place, and every hidden corner eagerly anticipate your arrival, ready to amaze and captivate you. Why spoil the thrill of that initial encounter, that overwhelming sense of awe? It's time to embrace the unparalleled excitement of becoming your own guide, where the boundaries are nonexistent, and your imagination becomes the sole means of transportation.

Unlike conventional guides, this book intentionally forgoes intricate maps. Why, you might wonder? Because we firmly believe that the most extraordinary discoveries transpire when you surrender to the unknown, when you allow yourself to get delightfully lost in the enigmatic charm of the surroundings. No predefined itineraries or rigid directions, for we yearn for you to immerse yourself in Kyoto on your own terms, free from boundaries or constraints. Surrender to the whims of exploration and uncover hidden treasures that no map could ever reveal. Dare to be bold, follow your instincts, and prepare to be astounded. The enchantment of this journey unfolds within your world, where roads materialize with each step, and the most astonishing adventures lie in the folds of the unknown. Embrace the magic that awaits you as you paint vivid images with your own eyes, for the truest and most beautiful pictures are the ones you create within your heart.

INTRODUCTION

In the realm of ancient beauty and cultural richness, Kyoto stands as a testament to Japan's profound history and captivating traditions. Nestled amidst serene temples, picturesque gardens, and enchanting tea houses, Kyoto transcends the boundaries of time, offering travelers an immersive experience like no other. As you embark on the journey through the pages of our meticulously crafted this guide get ready to unlock the secrets and soul of this timeless city.

Kyoto, Japan's former imperial capital, is a city that breathes history, exuding an aura of mystique that beckons visitors to explore its hallowed grounds. This guide is not merely a compendium of practical information; it is a key that opens doors to the heart and essence of Kyoto. Through vivid descriptions and expert insights, we aim to guide you beyond the tourist trail, allowing you to discover the hidden gems and cultural nuances that define this city.

What sets Kyoto apart is its harmonious blend of the old and the new, where ancient shrines and temples stand alongside modern innovations. It's a city where the echoes of samurai footsteps reverberate through narrow alleyways, and the delicate fragrance of cherry blossoms dances in the air during springtime. In our guide, we meticulously curate a journey that invites you to witness the intersection of tradition and innovation, ensuring you experience the city in its entirety.

As you leaf through the pages, you'll find detailed recommendations for must-visit landmarks, each with its unique story and significance. From the iconic Fushimi Inari Taisha, with its thousands of vermilion torii gates, to the sublime beauty of Kinkaku-ji, the Golden Pavilion, each destination is presented with historical context and cultural insights. We go beyond the surface, unraveling the tales woven into the fabric of Kyoto's architectural wonders.

But Kyoto is more than just a collection of landmarks; it's a city that thrives on its cultural heritage. Our guide delves into the intricacies of traditional tea ceremonies, the art of ikebana (flower arranging), and the mesmerizing world of geishas and maikos. Gain a deeper understanding of Kyoto's rich cultural tapestry, allowing you to engage with the city on a more profound level.

For the culinary enthusiasts, Kyoto's gastronomic landscape is a treasure trove of delights. From delectable kaiseki dining experiences to hidden gems serving local specialties, our guide navigates you through the flavors that define Kyoto's culinary identity. Savor the delicate tastes of matcha-flavored treats and indulge in the artistry of kaiseki chefs who transform meals into culinary masterpieces.

This guide is more than a roadmap; it's an invitation to immerse yourself in the soul-stirring beauty of Kyoto. Whether you're a seasoned traveler or a first-time visitor, our aim is to empower you to make the most of your Kyoto adventure. Join us as we embark on a journey through the heart of Japan's cultural gem, and let the guide be your companion in unraveling the secrets of this timeless city.

Brief History

Kyoto, the cultural heart of Japan, is a city that exudes history and tradition. Nestled in the central part of the island of Honshu, Kyoto served as the imperial capital of Japan for over a thousand years. This enduring legacy has shaped the city into a living museum, where ancient temples, traditional tea houses, and stunning gardens coexist with modern life. In this exploration of Kyoto's rich history, we will journey through the centuries to understand how this city has evolved and continues to play a crucial role in preserving Japan's cultural heritage.

Early Foundations (794–1185)
Kyoto's history as a capital city began in 794 when Emperor Kammu decided to move the imperial court from Nara to a new location. This relocation marked the establishment of Heian-kyo, the city that would eventually become Kyoto. The choice of location was not arbitrary; the site was carefully selected based on Chinese geomancy principles and the desire to distance the capital from the powerful Buddhist monasteries in Nara.

The Heian period (794–1185) saw the flourishing of aristocratic culture in Kyoto. The city became a center for literature, poetry, and courtly arts, with the Tale of Genji, written by Lady Murasaki Shikibu, being one of the most famous literary works from this era. Kyoto's layout reflected the Chinese capital, with a grid pattern of streets and the impressive Imperial Palace at its center.

Zen Buddhism and Samurai Era (1185–1603)
The Kamakura and Muromachi periods marked a shift in Kyoto's dynamics. Political power shifted from the imperial court to the military class, and Kyoto became a battleground for samurai warlords vying for control. Zen Buddhism gained prominence during this period, and iconic temples like Ryoan-ji and Tenryu-ji were founded.

The Onin War (1467–1477) devastated Kyoto, leading to a century of conflict and chaos known as the Warring States period. It wasn't until the rise of Oda Nobunaga, followed by

Toyotomi Hideyoshi and Tokugawa Ieyasu, that Japan began to experience a semblance of stability. However, the seat of political power eventually shifted to Edo (modern-day Tokyo) during the Tokugawa shogunate, marking the end of Kyoto's prominence as the political center.

Edo Period to Meiji Restoration (1603–1868)
The Edo period brought about a prolonged era of peace and stability, but Kyoto retained its cultural significance. The city became a hub for the arts, tea ceremonies, and traditional crafts. Kabuki theater thrived, and the Gion district emerged as the center of Kyoto's geisha culture.

The 19th century, however, brought significant upheaval. The arrival of Commodore Matthew Perry's fleet in 1853 forced Japan to open up to the outside world after centuries of isolation. The subsequent Meiji Restoration in 1868 aimed to modernize Japan, and the imperial capital was officially moved to Edo, renamed Tokyo.

Kyoto in the Modern Era (1868–Present)
Kyoto faced challenges during the Meiji period but managed to adapt and reinvent itself. The preservation of its cultural heritage became a key focus, and efforts were made to safeguard historic sites. The cityscape continued to evolve, with the introduction of modern infrastructure and industries.

During World War II, Kyoto was spared from the widespread bombing that targeted other Japanese cities, largely due to the efforts of the United States Secretary of War, Henry L. Stimson, who had a personal connection to the city and recognized its cultural importance. This preservation allowed Kyoto to emerge from the war with its historic treasures intact.

In the post-war period, Kyoto played a vital role in Japan's economic recovery. The city became a center for traditional arts, tourism, and education. The historic monuments of ancient Kyoto were collectively designated a UNESCO World Heritage Site in 1994, recognizing the city's unparalleled cultural significance.

Kyoto Today: Balancing Tradition and Modernity
In the 21st century, Kyoto continues to balance its rich history with the demands of modern life. The city is a juxtaposition of ancient temples and futuristic architecture. Traditional tea houses stand alongside trendy cafes, and the historic Gion district coexists with bustling shopping districts.

Kyoto's commitment to preserving its cultural heritage is evident in ongoing efforts to maintain historic sites, such as Kinkaku-ji (the Golden Pavilion) and Fushimi Inari Shrine. The city's traditional festivals, like Gion Matsuri, attract visitors from around the world, providing a glimpse into Japan's cultural tapestry.

The role of Kyoto extends beyond cultural preservation; it actively contributes to global discussions on sustainable living and environmental conservation. The city's commitment to preserving its natural surroundings and promoting eco-friendly practices aligns with the principles of traditional Japanese aesthetics, where harmony with nature is paramount.

Kyoto's history is a testament to the resilience of a city that has weathered centuries of change while preserving its cultural identity. From its origins as the imperial capital in the Heian period to its current status as a UNESCO World Heritage Site and a global cultural icon, Kyoto stands as a living embodiment of Japan's rich history and traditions. As the city navigates the challenges of the modern era, its ability to seamlessly integrate the past with the present ensures that Kyoto will continue to inspire awe and admiration for generations to come.

Why You Should Visit

Nestled in the heart of Japan, Kyoto stands as a living testament to the country's rich cultural heritage and historical significance. With its enchanting blend of traditional architecture, serene temples, and vibrant festivals, Kyoto is a must-visit destination for travelers seeking a glimpse into Japan's storied past. We delve into the myriad reasons why Kyoto beckons visitors from around the world, inviting them to immerse themselves in the unique charm of this ancient capital.

1. A Tapestry of Temples and Shrines: Spiritual Sanctuaries

Kyoto boasts a staggering array of temples and shrines, each contributing to the city's spiritual tapestry. Among these, the iconic Fushimi Inari Taisha takes center stage with its vermillion torii gates, creating a mesmerizing pathway up the sacred Mount Inari. Visitors can embark on a spiritual journey, winding through these gates and experiencing a sense of tranquility amidst the towering cedar trees.

The Golden Pavilion, Kinkaku-ji, is another jewel in Kyoto's crown. Covered in gold leaf, it reflects serenely on the waters of its surrounding pond, creating an otherworldly spectacle that captivates the hearts of all who behold it. The historic significance of these sites, coupled with their architectural brilliance, make Kyoto a haven for those seeking spiritual solace and cultural enrichment.

2. Cherry Blossoms in Bloom: A Symphony of Nature

Kyoto's cherry blossoms, or sakura, draw travelers in droves during the spring season. The ethereal beauty of these delicate pink blooms transforms the city into a fairy-tale landscape. Locals and tourists alike partake in "hanami" (flower viewing) picnics beneath the cherry blossom trees, creating a joyous atmosphere of celebration.

Maruyama Park, with its iconic weeping cherry tree, becomes a focal point for hanami enthusiasts. The ephemeral nature of the cherry blossoms serves as a poignant reminder of life's transience, fostering a deep appreciation for the present moment. For those seeking a sensory overload of color and fragrance, visiting Kyoto during cherry blossom season is an experience like no other.

3. Geisha Culture: Preserving Traditions in the Gion District

The Gion district stands as a living testament to Kyoto's commitment to preserving its cultural heritage. Famous for its traditional wooden machiya houses and cobbled streets, Gion is the epicenter of Kyoto's geisha culture. Visitors can catch a glimpse of geisha, known as geiko in Kyoto, gracefully making their way to appointments, adorned in exquisite kimonos and traditional white makeup.

Hanamachi, or geisha districts, are scattered throughout Kyoto, but Gion remains the most iconic. Witnessing a traditional geisha performance, known as a "maiko dance," provides a rare and enchanting glimpse into Japan's feudal past. The intricate rituals and artistry of geisha culture continue to thrive, making Gion a captivating destination for those intrigued by the elegance of a bygone era.

4. Historical Landmarks: Nijo Castle and Imperial Palace

Kyoto's landscape is dotted with historical landmarks that transport visitors to different eras of Japan's past. Nijo Castle, a UNESCO World Heritage Site, is renowned for its "nightingale floors" that chirp when walked upon, serving as a security measure against intruders. The castle's gardens, replete with cherry blossoms and seasonal foliage, offer a serene escape from the bustling city.

The Imperial Palace, with its sprawling gardens and majestic architecture, is another gem waiting to be explored. While the palace itself is not always open to the public, the surrounding East Gardens provide a tranquil setting for a leisurely stroll. These landmarks not only showcase Kyoto's architectural prowess but also serve as windows into the political and social fabric of Japan's past.

5. Culinary Delights: Kyoto Kaiseki and Matcha Madness

Kyoto's culinary scene is a gastronomic adventure, offering a unique blend of traditional and modern flavors. Kaiseki, a multi-course meal that reflects the changing seasons, is a culinary art form in Kyoto. Local ingredients are meticulously prepared and presented, creating a harmonious symphony of taste and texture.

For those with a sweet tooth, Kyoto is synonymous with matcha, a powdered green tea. Indulge in matcha-flavored treats, from delicate wagashi (traditional Japanese sweets) to matcha-infused ice cream. The city's teahouses, some nestled in the serene surroundings of temples, provide the perfect setting to savor the depth and richness of matcha while immersing yourself in the city's cultural ambiance.

6. Traditional Arts and Crafts: Kyoto's Artistic Legacy

Kyoto has long been a hub for traditional arts and crafts, preserving time-honored techniques passed down through generations. The Nishijin district, renowned for its silk weaving, allows visitors to witness the creation of intricate kimono fabrics. Kyoto's artisans also excel in the delicate art of Kyo-yuzen, a dyeing technique that adorns fabrics with vibrant, hand-painted designs.

The city's commitment to preserving these crafts is evident in the numerous workshops and galleries that offer hands-on experiences. Visitors can try their hand at pottery, calligraphy, or even the meticulous art of tea ceremony preparation. Kyoto's artistic legacy is a testament to the city's dedication to maintaining its cultural identity in a rapidly evolving world.

7. Seasonal Festivals: Matsuri Extravaganzas

Kyoto hosts a plethora of festivals throughout the year, each celebrating the changing seasons and ancient traditions. Gion Matsuri, one of Japan's most famous festivals, takes place in July and features vibrant processions of floats adorned with intricate tapestries. The Aoi Matsuri, held in May, is a grand spectacle where participants don medieval costumes and parade through the city.

These festivals offer a unique opportunity to witness Kyoto's streets come alive with color, music, and dance. Travelers can immerse themselves in the festive atmosphere, capturing the essence of Japan's celebratory spirit and the city's dynamic cultural calendar.

8. Tranquil Bamboo Forests: Arashiyama's Natural Beauty

Escape the urban hustle and bustle by venturing into the enchanting Arashiyama district, renowned for its bamboo groves and scenic landscapes. The Arashiyama Bamboo Grove provides a surreal experience as sunlight filters through the towering bamboo shoots, creating a play of light and shadow. Stroll through the pathways, and you'll feel transported to a mystical realm where nature and tranquility converge.

The Iwatayama Monkey Park, located in the same district, offers a unique opportunity to interact with Japanese macaques while enjoying panoramic views of Kyoto. Arashiyama's natural beauty provides a welcome respite, allowing visitors to connect with the serene side of Kyoto away from the historical sites and cultural attractions.

9. Scenic Gardens: Kyoto's Botanical Oases

Kyoto is dotted with meticulously landscaped gardens that offer an oasis of calm amidst the city's vibrant energy. The Ryoan-ji Temple's famous rock garden, with its meticulously arranged stones and raked gravel, is a prime example of the city's dedication to creating serene spaces for contemplation.

The Kyoto Imperial Palace Park, with its cherry blossom-lined paths, provides a picturesque setting for a leisurely stroll. Many of these gardens showcase traditional Japanese landscaping principles, incorporating elements such as ponds, bridges, and carefully manicured flora. These green havens offer visitors a chance to recharge and reflect in harmony with nature.

10. Accessibility and Connectivity: Gateway to Western Japan

Kyoto's strategic location makes it an ideal base for exploring the Kansai region and beyond. With efficient transportation options, including the shinkansen (bullet train), travelers can easily access nearby cities such as Osaka and Nara. Kyoto's central location makes it a gateway to the cultural richness and diverse landscapes that define western Japan.

Whether you're drawn to Kyoto for its cultural heritage, natural beauty, or culinary delights, the city's accessibility ensures that you can seamlessly explore the broader tapestry of Japan's wonders. From ancient traditions to modern marvels, Kyoto serves as a portal to the myriad facets of this captivating nation.

Kyoto stands as a city where the past seamlessly intertwines with the present, creating a tapestry of cultural richness that captivates the hearts of all who visit. From the spiritual sanctuaries of its temples and shrines to the mesmerizing beauty of cherry blossoms and the preservation of geisha culture, Kyoto offers a diverse array of experiences.

The city's commitment to traditional arts and crafts, its culinary delights, and the celebration of seasonal festivals contribute to Kyoto's timeless allure. As a gateway to western Japan, it beckons travelers to explore not only its storied streets but also the surrounding regions, each with its own unique charm.

Visiting Kyoto is not merely a journey through physical spaces; it's an immersive experience that transcends time, inviting you to connect with the essence of Japan's cultural identity. Whether you're a history enthusiast, a nature lover, or a culinary connoisseur, Kyoto promises a voyage of discovery, where every corner reveals a new facet of this ancient capital's enduring magic.

CHAPTER 1: Getting Started

Choosing the Right Time to Visit

Kyoto, with its rich history, cultural heritage, and breathtaking landscapes, is a city that captivates visitors throughout the year. However, the experience of exploring this ancient Japanese capital can vary significantly depending on the time of year. Whether you're drawn to cherry blossoms, vibrant festivals, or serene autumn foliage, selecting the right time to visit Kyoto is crucial for a truly immersive and memorable journey. We will delve into the distinct seasons and events that shape Kyoto's calendar, helping you make an informed decision on when to plan your visit.

Spring: Cherry Blossom Splendor (March to May)

For many, spring is the most enchanting season in Kyoto, marked by the ephemeral beauty of cherry blossoms, or "sakura." The city becomes a pastel wonderland, with iconic spots like Maruyama Park and the Philosopher's Path adorned with delicate pink blooms. Timing is crucial during this season, as cherry blossoms only last for a short period. Late March to early April is generally the peak bloom period, but it can vary based on weather conditions.

Besides enjoying the visual spectacle, spring is also an excellent time to partake in traditional Hanami parties, where locals and tourists alike gather under blooming cherry trees for picnics and celebrations. Keep in mind that spring is a popular tourist season, so be prepared for larger crowds and higher accommodation prices.

Summer: Festivals and Warm Evenings (June to August)

Summer in Kyoto brings a lively atmosphere with numerous festivals, known as "matsuri." The Gion Matsuri, held in July, is one of the most famous and features elaborate processions of floats, traditional performances, and vibrant street celebrations. The lively atmosphere continues into August with the Daimonji Gozan Okuribi, a spectacular event where massive bonfires are lit on mountainsides, creating mesmerizing patterns visible across the city.

While summer is marked by high temperatures and humidity, the evenings can be pleasant, providing an opportunity to explore the city after sunset. Be sure to pack accordingly for the warmer weather and consider participating in traditional summer activities like attending a Kyoto-style tea ceremony.

Autumn: Foliage and Tranquility (September to November)

Autumn in Kyoto is a painter's palette of reds, oranges, and golds as the city's foliage transforms into a breathtaking display. Popular spots for autumn foliage viewing include the Arashiyama Bamboo Grove, Kiyomizu-dera, and the Eikando Zenrinji Temple. The weather is generally mild, making it an ideal time for exploring both outdoor and indoor attractions.

September and November are particularly pleasant months, offering a tranquil atmosphere with fewer crowds compared to the peak cherry blossom season. Autumn also sees the arrival of seasonal culinary delights, such as chestnuts and sweet potatoes, adding an extra layer to your Kyoto experience.

Winter: Quiet Serenity and Cultural Experiences (December to February)

While winter is the coldest season in Kyoto, it offers a unique charm with fewer tourists and a serene atmosphere. The city's temples and shrines, dusted with a light layer of snow, create a picturesque scene. Winter is an excellent time to explore Kyoto's indoor attractions, including its many museums, traditional tea houses, and historic sites.

Additionally, winter marks the celebration of various cultural events, such as Hatsumode (New Year's shrine visit) and traditional mochitsuki (rice cake pounding) ceremonies. While the temperatures may be chilly, the festive spirit and cultural experiences make winter an appealing time to visit for those seeking a more intimate connection with Kyoto.

Considerations for Your Visit:

Crowds and Accommodation:

Peak tourist seasons (spring and autumn) often result in higher accommodation prices and larger crowds. Plan and book your stay well in advance to secure the best options.
If you prefer a quieter experience, consider visiting during the off-peak seasons (summer and winter).
Weather and Clothing:

Kyoto experiences four distinct seasons, so pack accordingly. Summers can be hot and humid, while winters can be cold. Layers are recommended, especially in spring and autumn when temperatures can vary throughout the day.
Cultural Events:

Check the calendar for major festivals and events happening during your visit. Participating in local traditions and celebrations can enhance your cultural experience.

Photography:

Each season in Kyoto offers unique photo opportunities. Consider your photography preferences and plan your visit around the visual elements you find most captivating.
Personal Preferences:

Consider your own preferences and interests when choosing the right time to visit. Whether you prioritize natural beauty, cultural events, or a more relaxed atmosphere, there is a season that aligns with your desires.

Choosing the right time to visit Kyoto involves a careful consideration of your preferences, interests, and the unique offerings of each season. Whether you're drawn to the ethereal beauty of cherry blossoms in spring, the vibrant festivals of summer, the picturesque foliage of autumn, or the serene tranquility of winter, Kyoto has something to offer year-round. By understanding the distinct characteristics of each season, you can tailor your visit to align with the experiences that resonate most with you, ensuring a truly unforgettable journey through this timeless city.

Getting to And Around

Kyoto, a city steeped in rich history and cultural significance, beckons travelers from around the world with its serene temples, traditional tea houses, and beautiful cherry blossoms. Navigating this ancient city requires a nuanced understanding of its transportation infrastructure, as well as an appreciation for its unique blend of modernity and tradition. We'll delve into the various ways of getting to and around Kyoto, ensuring that your visit is not only memorable but also hassle-free.

Getting to Kyoto
By Air
If you're arriving from overseas, Kansai International Airport
(KIX) is the primary gateway to Kyoto. Located
approximately 75 minutes away by train, KIX serves as a
major hub for international flights. Once you land, you can
take the Haruka Express, a direct train service connecting
the airport to Kyoto Station. Another option is Itami Airport
(ITM), primarily handling domestic flights. From Itami, a
bus or taxi can transport you to Kyoto in around 50 minutes.

By Train
Kyoto boasts excellent rail connections within Japan. The
Shinkansen, or bullet train, is a popular choice for those
traveling from Tokyo, Osaka, or other major cities. The
Tokaido Shinkansen connects Tokyo and Kyoto in just over
two hours, making it a convenient and efficient option. From
Osaka, the journey is even shorter, taking around 15 minutes
on the special rapid service on the JR Kyoto Line.

By Bus
Long-distance buses are another cost-effective means of
reaching Kyoto. Several companies operate overnight
services from major cities like Tokyo and Osaka. The journey
time can vary but generally takes around eight hours. Buses
arrive at the Kyoto Station or the Kyoto Bus Terminal, both
centrally located and well-connected to the city's public
transport network.

By Car
For those who prefer the flexibility of driving, Kyoto is
accessible by car. However, keep in mind that the city's
historic district has narrow streets, and parking can be
challenging. Renting a car is advisable for exploring the
surrounding areas, but for city exploration, public
transportation is more convenient.

Getting Around Kyoto

Public Transportation

Kyoto's public transportation system is both extensive and user-friendly. The city is served by buses, subways, and trains, offering a seamless way to explore its various districts. The Kyoto City Bus is a popular choice for tourists, with routes covering major attractions like Kinkaku-ji, Gion, and Fushimi Inari Shrine. A one-day bus pass allows unlimited rides, providing a cost-effective option for sightseeing.

The Kyoto Municipal Subway is another efficient mode of transportation, connecting key areas like Kyoto Station, Karasuma, and Kawaramachi. While the subway network is not as extensive as in some other cities, it is a convenient choice for specific routes.

Bicycles

Kyoto is a bicycle-friendly city, and renting a bike can be an excellent way to explore its quieter streets and hidden gems. Many rental shops offer hourly or daily rates, and the flat terrain makes cycling a pleasant experience. Biking allows you to discover the city at your own pace, giving you the freedom to stop and admire the scenery whenever you please.

Walking

One of the best ways to experience Kyoto's charm is on foot. Many of the city's attractions are within walking distance of each other, especially in the Higashiyama district, known for its historic streets and traditional architecture. Strolling through Gion, the famous geisha district, or along the Philosopher's Path, lined with cherry blossoms, provides an intimate and immersive experience of Kyoto's cultural heritage.

Taxis

Taxis are readily available in Kyoto, offering a more private and convenient option for those who prefer door-to-door service. While taxis can be more expensive than public transportation, they are a practical choice for reaching destinations not easily accessible by bus or train. Taxis can be hailed on the street or found at designated taxi stands throughout the city.

Ride-Sharing Apps
As of the last available information, ride-sharing services like Uber are not as prevalent in Kyoto as in some other cities. However, it's essential to check for any updates, as the availability of such services may have changed. Local taxi services and public transportation remain reliable options for getting around.

Navigating Kyoto's Attractions
Historical and Cultural Sites
Kyoto is renowned for its historic temples, shrines, and traditional tea houses. Navigating these attractions requires a combination of public transportation and walking. Many of the iconic sites, such as Kinkaku-ji (the Golden Pavilion) and Kiyomizu-dera, are accessible by bus or subway, followed by a short walk. Consider planning your itinerary to group attractions by proximity, optimizing your time and minimizing travel between sites.

Gion District
Exploring the Gion district, famous for its traditional wooden machiya houses and geisha culture, is best done on foot. Narrow cobblestone streets and charming tea houses create an enchanting atmosphere. The district is easily accessible from the city center and Kyoto Station by bus or taxi.

Fushimi Inari Shrine

Fushimi Inari Shrine, with its thousands of vermillion torii gates, is a must-visit attraction. Accessible by train and located just outside the JR Inari Station, the shrine is within walking distance. Be prepared for some uphill walking as you ascend the trails of Mount Inari, but the panoramic views make the effort worthwhile.

Arashiyama Bamboo Grove
To reach the Arashiyama Bamboo Grove, take the JR Sagano Line to Saga-Arashiyama Station. From there, it's a short walk to this ethereal bamboo forest. Consider combining your visit with other nearby attractions, such as the Iwatayama Monkey Park and the Togetsukyo Bridge, which spans the Hozu River.

Practical Tips for Navigating Kyoto
Transportation Passes
Consider purchasing transportation passes to save money and streamline your travel within Kyoto. The Kyoto City Bus and Kyoto Municipal Subway offer one-day and multiple-day passes that provide unlimited rides, allowing you to explore the city at your own pace. Additionally, the Japan Rail Pass is a cost-effective option for those planning to travel extensively within the country.

Navigational Apps
Utilize navigational apps to ease your exploration of Kyoto. Google Maps is a reliable choice, providing up-to-date information on public transportation schedules, walking routes, and estimated travel times. Local transport apps, such as the one provided by Kyoto City, can also be valuable resources for navigating the city.

Language Considerations
While English signage is prevalent in major tourist areas, it's beneficial to learn a few basic Japanese phrases for

navigating less frequented places. Politeness is highly valued in Japanese culture, and a simple "arigatou gozaimasu" (thank you) can go a long way in interactions with locals.

Peak Travel Times
Kyoto experiences peak tourist seasons, particularly during cherry blossom season in spring and the autumn foliage season. Plan your visit accordingly to avoid large crowds and ensure a more serene experience. Consider exploring popular attractions early in the morning or later in the afternoon to enjoy a quieter ambiance.

Accommodation Choice
Selecting accommodation close to public transportation hubs, such as Kyoto Station, can enhance your overall travel experience. This central location provides easy access to various modes of transportation, making it convenient for day trips and excursions to neighboring cities.

Navigating Kyoto is an adventure in itself, as you traverse through centuries of history and culture. Whether you're captivated by the iconic temples, enchanted by the historic districts, or savoring the tranquility of the bamboo groves, the city offers a myriad of experiences. By choosing the right modes of transportation and planning your itinerary thoughtfully, you'll uncover the hidden gems of Kyoto while immersing yourself in its timeless beauty.

Best Neighborhood to stay

Kyoto, with its rich history, stunning temples, and traditional tea houses, is a captivating destination for travelers seeking an authentic Japanese experience. Choosing the right neighborhood to stay in can greatly enhance your visit. We'll explore some of the best neighborhoods in Kyoto, each offering a unique blend of culture, convenience, and charm.

Higashiyama: Where Tradition Meets Modernity

Address: Higashiyama, Kyoto, Japan
Nestled in the eastern part of Kyoto, Higashiyama is renowned for its historic charm and narrow cobblestone streets. This neighborhood is home to some of Kyoto's most famous landmarks, including Kiyomizu-dera, Yasaka Shrine, and the charming Ninenzaka and Sannenzaka preserved districts. Traditional machiya houses line the streets, housing teahouses, shops, and local artisans. Staying in Higashiyama allows you to immerse yourself in Kyoto's traditional atmosphere while being within reach of modern amenities.

Gion: The Geisha District

Address: Gion, Kyoto, Japan
Gion is Kyoto's iconic geisha district, where traditional wooden machiya houses and upscale restaurants create a nostalgic ambiance. Hanami-koji Street, lined with tea houses and exclusive restaurants, is a great place for an evening stroll. Witnessing a geisha or maiko (apprentice geisha) walking gracefully to an engagement adds to the district's allure. Gion is perfect for those seeking an authentic and refined Kyoto experience.

Arashiyama: Nature and Tranquility
Address: Arashiyama, Kyoto, Japan
Located on the western outskirts of Kyoto, Arashiyama offers a peaceful retreat surrounded by nature. The famous Bamboo Grove, Iwatayama Monkey Park, and the historic Togetsukyo Bridge are some of the attractions that make this area special. Accommodations here often provide

picturesque views of the Hozugawa River and the lush Arashiyama mountains. For those wanting a break from the hustle and bustle, Arashiyama is an ideal choice.

Kyoto Station Area: Modernity and Connectivity

Address: Kyoto Station, Kyoto, Japan
The area around Kyoto Station is a hub of modernity, featuring high-end hotels, shopping complexes, and a multitude of dining options. Its central location makes it convenient for exploring both traditional and contemporary attractions in Kyoto. With direct access to various transportation options, including the Shinkansen, staying near Kyoto Station is ideal for those who prioritize convenience and efficient travel.

Fushimi: Sake and Shrines

Address: Fushimi, Kyoto, Japan
Fushimi, known for its sake breweries and the iconic Fushimi Inari Taisha Shrine, offers a unique blend of cultural and gastronomic experiences. The Fushimi Sake District allows visitors to sample a variety of sake brands, and the vibrant Torii gates leading to the shrine create a mesmerizing sight. If you're interested in Japanese spirits and spirituality, Fushimi is an excellent choice.

Nijo: Historical Residences and Gardens

Address: Nijo, Kyoto, Japan
Nijo, home to the famous Nijo Castle, provides a glimpse into Kyoto's feudal past. The castle, with its "nightingale floors" designed to chirp when walked upon, is a UNESCO World Heritage Site. The area around Nijo Castle is dotted with well-preserved machiya houses and beautiful gardens.

Staying in Nijo offers a serene and historically rich experience.

Pontocho: Riverside Dining and Entertainment

Address: Pontocho, Kyoto, Japan
Parallel to the Kamo River, Pontocho is a narrow alley filled with traditional tea houses, restaurants, and bars. In the evening, the lantern-lit street comes alive with the sounds of traditional music and dance. Pontocho offers a unique blend of riverside serenity and lively entertainment, making it an excellent choice for those seeking a vibrant nightlife scene.

Shimogyo: Shopping and Urban Vibes

Address: Shimogyo, Kyoto, Japan
Situated south of Kyoto Station, Shimogyo is a bustling commercial district offering a mix of modern shopping centers, department stores, and entertainment options. The iconic Kyoto Tower and the Kyoto Aquarium are prominent landmarks in this area. For travelers who enjoy urban exploration and want to be close to shopping and entertainment, Shimogyo is an attractive choice.

Choosing the right neighborhood in Kyoto depends on your preferences and the experiences you seek. Whether you prefer the historic charm of Higashiyama, the modern conveniences near Kyoto Station, or the tranquility of Arashiyama, each neighborhood has its own unique charm that adds to the overall allure of Kyoto. Consider your priorities and interests to make the most of your stay in this enchanting city.

Accommodation

Nestled in the heart of Japan, Kyoto stands as a testament to the country's rich cultural heritage and historical significance. Renowned for its well-preserved temples, traditional tea houses, and serene gardens, Kyoto attracts millions of visitors each year. To truly immerse oneself in the city's charm, selecting the right accommodation is paramount. This delves into the diverse options available for accommodation in Kyoto, from traditional ryokans to modern hotels, ensuring an unforgettable stay in this ancient capital.

Traditional Ryokans:

Kyoto's allure lies in its ability to transport visitors to a bygone era, and staying in a traditional ryokan is the perfect way to experience this cultural immersion. These Japanese inns are characterized by their tatami mat floors, sliding paper doors, and communal baths. One such gem is the Tawaraya Ryokan, a centuries-old establishment that seamlessly blends modern luxury with traditional aesthetics. Guests can savor kaiseki meals, sleep on futon bedding, and bask in the tranquil ambiance that pervades this enchanting ryokan.

Historic Machiya Stays:

For those seeking a more intimate connection with Kyoto's history, a machiya stay is a compelling option. Machiyas are traditional wooden townhouses that dot Kyoto's landscape, providing a unique glimpse into the city's architectural heritage. Some have been converted into cozy accommodations, such as the Machiya Residence Inn, where guests can relish the experience of living in a historic Japanese home while enjoying modern amenities.

Luxurious Hotels with a View:

Kyoto offers a range of luxurious hotels that cater to discerning travelers. The Ritz-Carlton Kyoto, perched along the Kamogawa River, provides a blend of opulence and Japanese elegance. With panoramic views of the Higashiyama Mountains, the hotel boasts spacious rooms, Michelin-starred dining, and a spa that integrates traditional Japanese wellness practices. The Four Seasons Hotel Kyoto is another five-star establishment, harmonizing modern luxury with Kyoto's cultural tapestry.

Budget-Friendly Hostels:

For the budget-conscious traveler, Kyoto doesn't fall short in providing affordable accommodation options. Hostels like the Kyoto Morris Hostel combine convenience with a social atmosphere. These hostels often offer dormitory-style rooms, communal spaces, and the chance to meet fellow travelers from around the world. The sense of camaraderie and shared experiences make these hostels an excellent choice for those looking to explore Kyoto on a shoestring budget.

Capsule Hotels for a Unique Experience:

For a truly unique and efficient stay, capsule hotels have become a popular choice in Kyoto. The 9 Hours Capsule Hotel provides compact yet comfortable sleeping pods, equipped with all the necessary amenities. This innovative concept ensures privacy while maximizing space utilization, making it an ideal option for solo travelers or those seeking a futuristic lodging experience.

Airbnb Options in Kyoto:

The rise of the sharing economy has made Airbnb a viable choice for accommodation in Kyoto. From traditional machiyas to modern apartments, Airbnb provides a diverse range of options that cater to various preferences and budgets. Staying in a local neighborhood allows visitors to experience daily life in Kyoto, offering a more authentic and immersive experience.

Choosing the Right Location:

Kyoto is divided into several districts, each with its unique charm. Choosing the right location for accommodation depends on individual preferences and the type of experience one seeks. Gion, known for its historic streets and geisha culture, is perfect for those wanting a taste of Kyoto's traditional ambiance. Downtown Kyoto, with its modern amenities and bustling atmosphere, appeals to those seeking a more contemporary experience.

Tips for Booking Accommodation:

Book Early: Kyoto is a popular tourist destination, and accommodations can fill up quickly, especially during peak seasons. Booking well in advance ensures a wider selection and often better rates.

Consider the Season: Kyoto experiences distinct seasons, each offering a different ambiance. Spring, with cherry blossoms in full bloom, is a favorite among visitors, while autumn showcases vibrant foliage. Be mindful of the season when planning your stay.

Read Reviews: Utilize online platforms and review websites to gauge the experiences of previous guests. This can provide valuable insights into the quality of accommodation, service, and amenities.

Transportation Accessibility: Consider the proximity of your chosen accommodation to public transportation, major attractions, and dining options. This ensures a convenient and efficient stay.

However, there are numerous apps for finding and booking accommodation at your convenience and disposal, catering for various budgets and preferences. Some of the most popular ones include the following:

Booking.com: Booking.com is a global platform that offers a wide range of accommodation options, including hotels, hostels, and apartments. It provides user reviews, detailed property information, and the ability to book directly through the app.

Airbnb: Airbnb is known for its diverse range of accommodation options, from private rooms to entire apartments or houses. It allows travelers to connect with local hosts and often provides a more personalized experience.

Expedia: Expedia is a comprehensive travel platform that not only offers accommodation but also provides options for booking flights, rental cars, and activities. It's a one-stop-shop for travel planning.

Agoda: Agoda specializes in offering accommodation options across Asia but has expanded its global presence. It often features competitive prices and deals on hotels and other lodging options.

Hotels.com: Hotels.com is a user-friendly app that provides a wide range of accommodation choices. It offers a loyalty program where users can earn free nights after a certain number of bookings.

Hostelworld: If you're looking for budget-friendly options like hostels, Hostelworld is a popular choice. It focuses on budget accommodations and is particularly useful for backpackers and solo travelers.

TripAdvisor: TripAdvisor is a well-known platform that offers reviews and ratings for hotels, restaurants, and attractions. It also allows users to book accommodation directly through the app.

Hopper: While primarily known for its flight predictions and booking features, Hopper has expanded its services to include hotel bookings. It often provides insights into the best times to book for optimal savings.

Trivago: Trivago is a hotel search and price comparison app that aggregates deals from various booking sites. It allows users to compare prices and find the best deals on accommodations.

HomeAway: HomeAway, now part of the Vrbo family, focuses on vacation rentals and is an excellent choice if you're looking for a home-like experience during your stay.

Instead of recommending hotels, Vacation rentals, guesthouses, resorts etc, as the case may be, we believe every traveler should have the liberty to make use of this apps to chose the accommodation of their choice because;
Everyone has different preferences when it comes to accommodations. Some may prefer the luxury and amenities of a hotel, while others might opt for the authenticity of a local guesthouse or the privacy of a vacation rental. Choosing your own accommodation allows you to align your stay with your specific preferences and needs.

Accommodation costs can vary widely, and travelers may have specific budget constraints. By selecting their own accommodation, travelers can explore a range of options that fit their budget, whether it's a budget-friendly hostel, a mid-range hotel, or a high-end luxury resort.

The location of your accommodation can significantly impact your travel experience. Travelers often have specific preferences regarding proximity to attractions, public transportation, or specific neighborhoods. Choosing your own accommodation allows you to select a location that suits your itinerary and preferences.

Staying in local guesthouses, boutique hotels, or vacation rentals can offer a more immersive cultural experience. These accommodations often reflect the local architecture, design, and lifestyle, providing a deeper connection to the destination.

Some travelers value personalized experiences that are not always available in standard hotels. Bed and breakfasts, boutique hotels, and guesthouses often provide a more intimate atmosphere, with personalized attention and local insights from the hosts.

Accommodation preferences often extend to the amenities offered. Some travelers prioritize fitness facilities, while others may value a fully equipped kitchen, free Wi-Fi, or pet-friendly policies. Choosing your own accommodation allows you to prioritize the amenities that matter most to you.

Travelers celebrating special occasions, such as anniversaries or birthdays, may want to choose accommodations that offer a more romantic or celebratory atmosphere. Some hotels and resorts provide special packages for such occasions.

Unique accommodations, such as historic inns, treehouses, or houseboats, can contribute to a memorable and authentic travel experience. Choosing unconventional lodgings allows travelers to step outside the conventional hotel experience.

Travelers have the flexibility to choose from a variety of booking platforms based on their preferences. Whether using popular booking websites, directly booking through the accommodation's website, or utilizing alternative lodging platforms, the choice is in the hands of the traveler.

Being actively involved in the accommodation selection process can instill confidence and peace of mind. Reading reviews, viewing photos, and understanding the accommodation's policies contribute to a sense of control and assurance in your travel plans.

Many of these booking apps provides reviews, ratings and recommendation for properties. These feedbacks helps travelers make an informed decisions on where to stay. It empowers them to avoid potential risks and issues and choose accommodation that align with their preferences.

Kyoto's accommodation options cater to a diverse range of preferences, from those seeking traditional Japanese experiences to modern luxury. The city's unique blend of history and modernity is reflected in its lodgings, ensuring that every visitor can find a place that resonates with their vision of an ideal stay. Whether it's the immersive tranquility of a ryokan, the historic charm of a machiya, or the contemporary comforts of a luxury hotel, choosing the right accommodation enhances the overall experience of exploring Kyoto, allowing visitors to create lasting memories in Japan's ancient capital.

Chapter 2: Landmarks and Attractions

Kyoto, the ancient capital of Japan, is a city that encapsulates the essence of Japanese history, culture, and tradition. Steeped in rich heritage, Kyoto boasts a myriad of landmarks and attractions that draw millions of visitors each year. From stunning temples and shrines to picturesque gardens and historic districts, the city offers a captivating journey through time. We'll delve into the must-visit landmarks and attractions in Kyoto, providing you with insights into their historical significance, architectural beauty, and cultural importance.

Kinkaku-ji (The Golden Pavilion)

Address: 1 Kinkakujicho, Kita Ward, Kyoto, 603-8361, Japan

Kinkaku-ji, also known as the Golden Pavilion, stands as a radiant jewel in Kyoto's cultural crown, captivating visitors with its unparalleled beauty and historical significance. Nestled in the northern part of Kyoto in Kita Ward, the temple's address is 1 Kinkakujicho, Kyoto, 603-8361, Japan.

Constructed in the 14th century, Kinkaku-ji has a fascinating origin that adds to its allure. Initially, it was not intended to be a religious sanctuary but rather served as a retirement villa for Ashikaga Yoshimitsu, a powerful shogun of the Ashikaga shogunate. The shogun's vision for this retreat was one of opulence and tranquility, reflected in the architectural masterpiece that we see today.

The Golden Pavilion's distinctive exterior is a testament to the artistic prowess of its time. The upper two floors are adorned with sheets of pure gold leaf, creating a dazzling spectacle that seems to shimmer in the sunlight. This golden exterior is not merely for decorative purposes; it symbolizes the pursuit of enlightenment, reflecting the Zen Buddhist philosophy that underpins the temple's spiritual essence.

One of the most captivating aspects of Kinkaku-ji is its reflection in the tranquil waters of the surrounding pond, known as Kyoko-chi (Mirror Pond). The mirror-like surface not only amplifies the brilliance of the golden exterior but also adds an ethereal quality to the entire setting. Visitors often find themselves enchanted by the interplay of light and water, creating a visual poetry that leaves a lasting impression.

The meticulously landscaped gardens surrounding Kinkaku-ji further elevate the temple's overall charm. The grounds, known as the Rokuon-ji Garden, are carefully designed to harmonize with the natural environment, featuring scenic walking paths, vibrant foliage, and strategically placed stones. The teahouse, Fudo-an, situated within the garden, offers a serene spot for contemplation, allowing visitors to absorb the tranquility that permeates the entire area.

Each season brings a new dimension to the beauty of Kinkaku-ji. In spring, cherry blossoms frame the golden pavilion with delicate pink hues, creating a scene reminiscent of a traditional Japanese painting. Summer transforms the surrounding greenery into a lush embrace, while autumn bathes the temple in the warm tones of red and gold foliage. Even in winter, a subtle charm graces the temple, with a dusting of snow adding a quiet elegance to the landscape.

Beyond its aesthetic appeal, Kinkaku-ji holds a deeper spiritual significance. It is an active Zen Buddhist temple of the Rinzai sect, fostering a connection between the past and the present. Visitors can explore the interiors of the temple, adorned with exquisite artwork and artifacts, gaining insights into the historical and religious aspects that define Kinkaku-ji.

In essence, Kinkaku-ji stands as a living testament to the delicate balance between human artistry and nature's beauty, between worldly opulence and spiritual enlightenment. As visitors wander through its hallowed grounds and marvel at the golden facade that has withstood the test of time, they partake in a journey that transcends the boundaries of centuries, immersing themselves in the timeless allure of Kyoto's most iconic landmark.

Fushimi Inari Taisha

Address: 68 Fukakusa Yabunouchicho, Fushimi Ward, Kyoto, 612-0882, Japan

Nestled in the heart of Kyoto, Fushimi Inari Taisha stands as a cultural beacon, drawing pilgrims, tourists, and seekers alike to its captivating grounds. The shrine, dedicated to Inari, the Shinto god of rice and prosperity, has become synonymous with its iconic feature—the vibrant torii gate pathway. The address, 68 Fukakusa Yabunouchicho, Fushimi Ward, Kyoto, 612-0882, Japan, unveils the location of this sacred sanctuary.

The defining feature of Fushimi Inari Taisha is undoubtedly the seemingly infinite rows of torii gates, painted in a brilliant vermilion hue. As visitors approach the shrine's entrance, they are welcomed by a breathtaking tunnel of these iconic gates, creating a corridor of color and mystique.

Each gate, known as a "torii," is generously donated by individuals and businesses seeking blessings and prosperity. This act of dedication adds a personal touch to the already spiritual ambiance of the shrine.

The journey through the torii gate pathway is symbolic, representing a passage from the mundane to the sacred. Walking beneath the vermillion arches, visitors embark on a spiritual odyssey that transcends the physical realm. The mesmerizing tunnel of gates continues for approximately 2.5 miles, leading pilgrims and explorers through a lush forested area up the slopes of Mount Inari. The gentle rustle of leaves, accompanied by the occasional chime of a temple bell, creates a serene symphony that enhances the overall experience.

Beyond the initial torii gate tunnel, the ascent to the main shrine on Mount Inari unfolds. Many visitors choose to undertake the hike, a journey that takes approximately 2-3 hours to complete. Along the way, smaller shrines, known as "sub-shrines," dot the landscape. These sub-shrines serve as resting points and provide moments of quiet reflection. Each one is uniquely adorned and holds its own spiritual significance, contributing to the rich tapestry of Fushimi Inari Taisha.

The panoramic views of Kyoto from various vantage points along the mountain trail are nothing short of awe-inspiring. As visitors ascend, they are treated to glimpses of the city's rooftops, traditional temples, and the meandering Kamo River. The harmonious blend of nature and urbanity is a testament to the thoughtful placement of Fushimi Inari Taisha, providing a spiritual retreat within the embrace of Kyoto's bustling surroundings.

The main shrine, situated at the summit of Mount Inari, is a culmination of the spiritual journey. Its architectural grandeur and intricate details pay homage to Inari, the revered deity. Visitors often offer prayers and make symbolic gestures of respect, immersing themselves in the solemnity of the sacred space. The panoramic view from the summit further accentuates the sense of accomplishment and connection with the divine.

Fushimi Inari Taisha, with its vibrant torii gate pathway and spiritual ascent to Mount Inari, encapsulates the essence of Shinto beliefs and Japanese reverence for nature. The blend of spirituality and natural beauty creates an experience that transcends the ordinary, leaving an indelible mark on those who traverse its sacred grounds. In every torii gate, there is a whisper of prayers, a touch of history, and an invitation to explore the profound connection between the spiritual and the sublime.

Kiyomizu-dera

Address: 294 Kiyomizu, Higashiyama Ward, Kyoto, 605-0862, Japan
Nestled atop the eastern hills of Kyoto, Kiyomizu-dera stands as a testament to architectural ingenuity and natural beauty. As one of Kyoto's most revered landmarks, this UNESCO World Heritage Site has been enchanting visitors for centuries with its breathtaking panoramas and cultural significance.

The main hall, a marvel in itself, is a testament to the craftsmanship of the Edo period. What sets it apart is the absence of nails in its construction, showcasing the meticulous engineering prowess of the time. This structural feat not only adds an element of historical intrigue but also contributes to the serene ambiance that permeates the temple grounds.

A Perilous View:

The defining feature of Kiyomizu-dera is its wooden terrace, known as the "Kiyomizu-no-Butai" or Kiyomizu Stage, extending out over the hillside with no visible support from below. Suspended above the valley, this terrace offers a dizzying yet awe-inspiring view of Kyoto's urban sprawl. The name Kiyomizu, translating to "clear water," originates from the Otowa Waterfall within the complex, where visitors can drink from three separate streams, each believed to grant a specific virtue - longevity, success in academics, and a fortunate love life.

Cherry Blossom Elegance:

While Kiyomizu-dera is a year-round attraction, it takes on a special charm during the cherry blossom season. The terrace, adorned with cherry blossom trees, transforms into a sea of delicate pink petals, creating a surreal and romantic atmosphere. The juxtaposition of the ancient wooden structure against the ephemeral beauty of cherry blossoms is a sight to behold, attracting both locals and tourists seeking the quintessential Kyoto spring experience.

Maple-Covered Vistas:

In the fall, the temple undergoes another metamorphosis as the surrounding maple trees erupt in vibrant hues of red and gold. The terrace becomes a vantage point for witnessing the fiery spectacle of autumn, with the cityscape below painted in warm tones. The Japanese concept of "momijigari," or maple viewing, finds its perfect setting at Kiyomizu-dera during this season.

Cultural Significance:

Beyond its scenic grandeur, Kiyomizu-dera holds deep cultural and religious significance. Dedicated to the Kannon Bodhisattva, the goddess of mercy, the temple has been a place of worship since its establishment in 778. The various halls and pagodas within the complex house sacred artifacts and religious icons, providing visitors with a glimpse into the spiritual heart of Japan.

The Otowa Waterfall:

Descending through the complex, the Otowa Waterfall is a spiritual focal point. Visitors can use cups attached to long poles to catch and drink the pure, flowing water, believed to bestow blessings upon those who partake. The ritual of drinking from the three streams is a meditative experience, connecting visitors with the temple's sacred history.

In essence, Kiyomizu-dera is not merely a temple; it is an immersive journey into Japan's cultural and natural treasures. Its architectural marvels, seasonal transformations, and spiritual resonance make it a must-visit destination for anyone seeking to unravel the layers of Kyoto's profound heritage. Whether you're drawn to its perilous views, symbolic rituals, or simply the tranquility it exudes, Kiyomizu-dera invites you to embrace the essence of Japan's spiritual and aesthetic splendor.

Arashiyama Bamboo Grove

Address: Ukyo Ward, Kyoto, 616-0007, Japan

Nestled within the Arashiyama district in Kyoto, the Bamboo Grove is a captivating testament to the sublime beauty of nature. A visit to this ethereal landscape offers an immersive experience as you find yourself surrounded by towering bamboo stalks that create a mesmerizing natural canopy. The sheer scale and density of the bamboo forest make it a visual spectacle, transporting visitors to a realm that feels otherworldly.

Nature's Canopy: A Visual Extravaganza

The Arashiyama Bamboo Grove stands as one of Kyoto's most iconic and photographed locations, drawing visitors from around the world to witness its enchanting beauty. As you enter the grove, you're immediately enveloped by the soothing rustle of bamboo leaves swaying in the breeze. The slender, towering bamboo shoots reach towards the sky, creating a sense of awe and wonder. The play of light filtering through the dense bamboo canopy adds an ethereal quality to the surroundings, casting intricate shadows on the forest floor.

Tranquility Amidst Giants

Beyond its visual appeal, the Bamboo Grove offers a serene and tranquil atmosphere. The tall bamboo stalks create a natural barrier, muffling the sounds from the outside world and fostering a sense of peace and isolation. Visitors often find themselves immersed in a meditative state as they wander through the meandering paths, with the occasional shaft of sunlight breaking through the bamboo leaves, creating a serene interplay of light and shadow.

Tenryu-ji Temple: A Cultural Oasis

Adjacent to the Bamboo Grove lies the renowned Tenryu-ji Temple, a UNESCO World Heritage Site that enhances the overall allure of the Arashiyama district. Founded in the 14th century, this Zen temple boasts exquisite gardens that complement the natural beauty of the bamboo forest. The temple's architecture harmoniously blends with the surrounding landscape, offering visitors a seamless transition from the ethereal bamboo environment to the tranquility of the temple grounds.

Togetsukyo Bridge: Bridging Nature and Architecture

As you explore the Arashiyama district, the iconic Togetsukyo Bridge emerges as a symbol of harmony between nature and human craftsmanship. Spanning the Hozugawa River, this picturesque bridge provides panoramic views of the bamboo-clad hills and the surrounding landscape. The name "Togetsukyo" translates to "Moon Crossing Bridge," a poetic nod to the breathtaking moonlit reflections in the river below, making it a must-visit spot during both day and night.

Seasonal Splendor: A Year-Round Delight

While the Arashiyama Bamboo Grove is a perennial attraction, each season brings its own enchanting transformation. Spring bathes the grove in a soft palette of cherry blossoms, creating a delicate contrast against the vibrant green bamboo. Summer sees the bamboo forest at its lushest, with the rustling leaves providing a cool respite from the heat. Autumn transforms the landscape into a tapestry of reds and golds, while winter lends a serene charm with a dusting of snow on the bamboo.

The Arashiyama Bamboo Grove is not merely a destination; it's an immersive journey into nature's grandeur and tranquility. From the towering bamboo stalks creating a natural cathedral to the adjacent cultural gems like Tenryu-ji Temple and the poetic Togetsukyo Bridge, this enchanting corner of Kyoto invites visitors to step out of reality and into a world where the beauty of the natural and human-made coalesce in harmonious splendor.

Gion District

Address: Gion, Higashiyama Ward, Kyoto, Japan

The Gion District in Kyoto stands as an enchanting gateway to the city's rich historical legacy, preserving the essence of traditional Japan amidst the modern urban landscape. Situated in the Higashiyama Ward, Gion is a living testament to Kyoto's enduring charm, attracting visitors with its well-preserved wooden machiya houses, iconic geisha culture, and a captivating ambiance that transports you back in time.

One of the defining features of Gion is its narrow cobblestone streets that wind their way through the district, creating an intimate and timeless atmosphere. As you wander through these charming pathways, you'll find yourself surrounded by wooden facades adorned with delicate latticework, offering a glimpse into the architectural aesthetics of a bygone era. The traditional machiya houses, with their distinct gabled roofs and sliding paper doors, contribute to the authentic charm of Gion, making it a visually arresting district that seems to have resisted the relentless march of time.

Tea houses, or "ochaya," and traditional ryokan inns are scattered throughout Gion, adding to the district's allure. These establishments provide a window into Japan's age-old hospitality traditions, where guests can experience the art of the tea ceremony or enjoy the tranquility of a Japanese-style inn. Many of these establishments have been meticulously preserved, allowing visitors to step into a world where time seems to stand still, offering a respite from the fast-paced nature of modern life.

Hanami-koji Street, one of Gion's most famous thoroughfares, is a focal point of the district's allure. As day transitions into night, the lantern-lit street takes on a magical quality, creating an ambiance that is both romantic and nostalgic. Here, the air is filled with the subtle rustle of silk and the gentle click-clack of traditional wooden sandals as geisha and maiko move gracefully between engagements. Hanami-koji Street is renowned as a prime spot for encountering these iconic figures, and with luck, visitors may catch a glimpse of them on their way to entertain guests in the ochaya.

Geisha, known for their mastery of traditional arts such as dance, music, and the tea ceremony, have long been a symbol of Kyoto's cultural heritage. Gion, as the epicenter of the city's geisha culture, provides a rare opportunity to witness these artisans in their element. The ethereal beauty of geisha and the apprentice maiko, with their elaborate kimonos and distinctive hairstyles, adds a layer of mystique to Gion, further enhancing its timeless appeal.

Beyond its visual splendor, Gion offers a profound connection to Kyoto's cultural past. The district's history is interwoven with tales of samurai, artists, and nobility who once strolled through its streets. In Gion, every building, every stone, and every step echoes with the whispers of centuries past, allowing visitors to immerse themselves in the city's cultural tapestry.

In essence, a visit to Gion is not merely a stroll through a historic district; it is a journey back in time, a nostalgic exploration of Kyoto's cultural soul. As one meanders through its cobblestone streets, surrounded by the rustic charm of machiya houses and the alluring presence of geisha, Gion unveils the layers of history that have shaped Kyoto into the cultural gem it is today. It is a place where tradition and modernity harmonize, inviting visitors to partake in the enduring beauty of Japan's past.

Nijo Castle

Address: 541 Nijojocho, Nakagyo Ward, Kyoto, 604-8301, Japan

Nestled in the heart of Kyoto's Nakagyo Ward, Nijo Castle stands as a testament to the grandeur and sophistication of Japan's feudal era. Designated as a UNESCO World Heritage Site, this architectural masterpiece invites visitors to step back in time to the 17th century when it served as the residence of Tokugawa shoguns. The castle, with its distinctive features and historical significance, offers a captivating journey into Japan's rich cultural heritage.

One of the most enchanting aspects of Nijo Castle is its ingenious "nightingale floors." As visitors explore the corridors of the Ninomaru Palace, the floors emit a soft, melodic chirping sound reminiscent of a nightingale's song. This acoustic security feature, designed to alert occupants to any approaching intruders, adds an element of intrigue and charm to the castle. The rhythmic symphony of the floors is a living testament to the ingenious engineering prowess of the past.

The castle complex itself is a harmonious blend of architectural brilliance and natural beauty. The Ninomaru Palace, in particular, stands out as a gem within the vast grounds. This palace, designated as a National Treasure of Japan, boasts exquisite wall paintings that narrate tales of nature, folklore, and historical events. As visitors traverse the meticulously crafted corridors and rooms, they are transported to an era where the elite lived surrounded by opulence and cultural refinement.

The Ninomaru Palace's interiors are adorned with intricate details, showcasing the craftsmanship of the Edo period. Sliding doors with delicate gold leaf designs, intricately painted screens, and beautifully crafted transoms contribute to the overall aesthetic richness of the palace. The "Kara-mon" gate, an elaborate entrance adorned with Chinese motifs, welcomes visitors into the palace grounds, setting the tone for the opulence that awaits within.

Surrounding the palace, Nijo Castle's expansive gardens provide a serene backdrop to the historical grandeur. The gardens, designed in the traditional Japanese style, feature meticulously manicured landscapes, serene ponds, and vibrant flora that change with the seasons. Cherry blossoms in spring and fiery maple leaves in autumn enhance the beauty of the surroundings, creating a picturesque setting for visitors to explore and enjoy.

As one explores Nijo Castle, the historical resonance of the site becomes palpable. The "Higashi Ote-mon" and "Karamon" gates, both designated Important Cultural Properties, serve as impressive architectural remnants of a bygone era. The "Seiryu-en" garden, added in the modern era, complements the historic elements with contemporary landscaping, creating a harmonious blend of old and new.

Visiting Nijo Castle is not merely a glimpse into the past; it is a sensory experience that immerses visitors in the sights and sounds of a bygone era. The meticulous preservation of the castle and its grounds ensures that each step within its confines is a step back in time. From the creaking of the nightingale floors to the breathtaking artistry of the Ninomaru Palace, Nijo Castle invites guests to appreciate the cultural legacy of Kyoto and the nation as a whole.

Nijo Castle stands as a living monument to Japan's historical opulence and architectural ingenuity. With its "nightingale floors," lavish interiors, and enchanting gardens, the castle beckons travelers to explore the rich tapestry of Japan's feudal past. As the sun sets over the castle's towers and gardens, the echoes of centuries past linger, inviting all who visit to become part of the enduring story of Nijo Castle.

Kyoto Imperial Palace

Address: 3 Kyotogyoen, Kamigyo Ward, Kyoto, 602-0881, Japan

Nestled within the heart of Kyoto, the Kyoto Imperial Palace stands as a testament to the imperial legacy that once graced the city. This grand complex, encompassed by picturesque gardens and vast open spaces, served as the residence of the Imperial family until the shifting tides of history prompted the capital's relocation to Tokyo. While the regal interiors of the palace remain largely inaccessible to the public, the surrounding Kyoto Imperial Park offers a serene oasis for those seeking a glimpse into Japan's imperial past.

The Imperial Palace, with its rich history dating back centuries, is a symbol of continuity and change. The sprawling grounds are enveloped by meticulously manicured gardens, creating an ambiance of tranquility that contrasts with the city's bustling exterior. It's a place where time seems to slow down, allowing visitors to connect with the imperial heritage that shaped Kyoto's identity.

As you enter the precincts of the palace, the first thing that captures your attention is the expansive Kyoto Imperial Park that stretches before you. The park is a canvas of greenery, adorned with cherry and plum trees that burst into a riot of color during the springtime cherry blossom season. It's a favored spot for locals and tourists alike to partake in the centuries-old tradition of hanami, or flower viewing, under the fragrant blooms.

While the palace buildings themselves remain reserved for official functions and ceremonies, the opportunity to stroll around the exterior is a unique and enriching experience. The grandeur of the walls and gates, constructed with meticulous attention to detail, transports visitors to an era where emperors and empresses once walked these hallowed grounds. The Otemon Gate, with its distinctive vermilion color, is a particularly striking feature that stands as a sentinel to the palace's historic significance.

Every corner of the palace grounds whispers tales of the past. The Seiryoden, a building within the palace complex, served as the residence of the Emperor during the Heian period. Though not accessible to the public, its elegant architectural features and the surrounding gardens provide a glimpse into the opulence and refinement of imperial life.

For those with a penchant for history, the Sento Imperial Palace within the same grounds offers guided tours, providing deeper insights into the imperial lifestyle. The tours unravel the layers of history hidden within the palace walls, shedding light on the ceremonies and rituals that were once integral to court life.

As the sun sets and casts a warm glow over the palace grounds, the ambiance becomes truly magical. The expansive lawns, meticulously pruned trees, and ancient stone pathways create an ethereal setting for an evening stroll. It's a time when the whispers of history are most audible, and one can almost sense the echoes of the imperial past resonating through the air.

In essence, the Kyoto Imperial Palace and its surrounding park offer more than just a visit; they provide a gateway to a bygone era. The allure lies not only in the tangible structures but also in the intangible connection to the traditions and legacy that have shaped Japan's imperial history. As you navigate the pathways and absorb the serene beauty, the Kyoto Imperial Palace becomes not just a destination but a living chronicle of the grace and grandeur of Japan's imperial heritage.

Ryoan-ji Temple

Address: 13 Ryoanji Goryonoshitacho, Ukyo Ward, Kyoto, 616-8001, Japan

Nestled in the Ukyo Ward of Kyoto, Ryoan-ji Temple stands as a testament to the artistry of simplicity and the profound impact it can have on the human spirit. This Zen Buddhist temple, founded in the late 15th century during the Muromachi period, has garnered global acclaim for its iconic rock garden – a masterpiece of minimalist design that elevates the act of contemplation to an art form.

The Essence of Ryoan-ji's Rock Garden
The heart of Ryoan-ji's allure lies in its rock garden, one of the most celebrated examples of karesansui, or dry landscape gardens, in Japan. As visitors enter the temple grounds, they are greeted by a rectangular plot of meticulously raked gravel adorned with 15 carefully placed rocks. However, what makes this garden exceptional is the deliberate arrangement of the stones and the absence of any flora.

The stark simplicity of Ryoan-ji's rock garden is deliberate, inviting contemplation and introspection. The gravel itself is raked in precise, flowing patterns that add to the meditative ambiance. The lack of explicit symbolism or narrative in the arrangement prompts visitors to explore their own interpretations, fostering a unique and personal connection with the garden.

The Zen Philosophy of Ryoan-ji
Ryoan-ji Temple encapsulates the essence of Zen philosophy, emphasizing the beauty found in simplicity, impermanence, and the importance of living in the present moment. The deliberate lack of adornments allows visitors to strip away distractions, focusing on the rocks and gravel as metaphors for the impermanence of life and the continuous flow of time.

The contemplative atmosphere is enhanced by the surrounding architecture, including the Hojo, the head priest's former residence. This traditional building provides a serene backdrop to the garden, emphasizing the harmonious coexistence of nature and human craftsmanship.

Cultural Significance and Historical Roots
Founded in 1488 by Hosokawa Katsumoto, a powerful military leader of the time, Ryoan-ji Temple has witnessed centuries of historical events while maintaining its timeless serenity. Despite being partially destroyed during the Onin War in the 15th century, the temple was meticulously reconstructed to preserve its architectural and spiritual significance.

Over the centuries, Ryoan-ji has become a sanctuary for those seeking solace and a deeper connection with themselves. The temple's influence extends beyond its physical boundaries, as the concept of the rock garden has inspired artists, architects, and philosophers worldwide.

Visitor Experience and Contemplative Practice

Upon entering the temple grounds, visitors are required to remove their shoes before stepping onto the wooden veranda that surrounds the rock garden. This act not only symbolizes a physical detachment from the external world but also serves as a gesture of respect for the sacred space within.

As visitors gaze upon the carefully arranged stones, a profound sense of calm washes over them. The act of contemplation becomes a personal journey, with each individual drawing their own conclusions about the meaning behind the arrangement. The tranquil environment and lack of explicit guidance encourage a form of meditation unique to each person's state of mind.

Preservation and Future Generations
Recognizing the cultural and historical significance of Ryoan-ji Temple, efforts have been made to ensure its preservation for future generations. The temple is designated as a UNESCO World Heritage Site, underscoring its importance not only in the context of Japanese heritage but also on a global scale.

As Ryoan-ji continues to welcome visitors from around the world, its timeless message of simplicity, contemplation, and the beauty inherent in the present moment remains as relevant as ever. The rocks in the garden, seemingly frozen in time, serve as silent witnesses to the passage of centuries, inviting each visitor to embrace the fleeting nature of existence and find serenity in the ever-flowing currents of life.

Kyoto International Manga Museum

Address: Karasuma-Oike, Nakagyo Ward, Kyoto, 604-0846, Japan

Nestled in the heart of Kyoto, where tradition meets modernity, the Kyoto International Manga Museum stands as a testament to the evolving cultural landscape of the city. This unique museum, with its unassuming exterior, opens up a world of creativity and imagination, showcasing the vibrant art form of manga.

A Haven for Manga Aficionados
With a vast collection exceeding 300,000 manga, the museum is a haven for manga enthusiasts and casual readers alike. The shelves stretch as far as the eye can see, housing a comprehensive array of manga genres, from classic to contemporary, shonen to shojo. The sheer diversity of the collection caters to all tastes, ensuring that every visitor can find something that resonates with them.

Unleashing the Power of Accessibility
What sets the Kyoto International Manga Museum apart is its innovative approach to accessibility. Unlike traditional museums where exhibits are sealed behind glass, this institution encourages visitors to immerse themselves in the world of manga. The shelves, lined with neatly arranged manga volumes, invite patrons to freely peruse and explore the artistry and narratives within. It's a hands-on experience that bridges the gap between creators and readers, fostering a unique connection between the art and its audience.

Borrowing Culture: A Literary Adventure

The museum takes the concept of a traditional library and infuses it with the dynamic spirit of manga. Visitors have the extraordinary opportunity to borrow manga from the shelves and find a cozy spot within the museum's reading areas. Whether it's a secluded corner bathed in natural light or a communal space buzzing with fellow manga enthusiasts, the reading environment caters to diverse preferences. This borrowing culture extends beyond the museum's walls, as patrons can take their selected manga to the nearby park or a local café, creating a literary adventure that transcends the conventional museum experience.

A Celebration of Manga's Cultural Significance
Beyond its role as a repository for manga, the museum serves a higher purpose – celebrating the cultural significance of this art form. Manga is not merely a source of entertainment but a powerful medium that reflects societal trends, historical narratives, and the evolving perspectives of its creators. The museum curates special exhibitions and events that delve into the deeper layers of manga culture, exploring its impact on Japanese society and its global influence.

Interactive Workshops and Events
To further engage visitors, the Kyoto International Manga Museum organizes a variety of workshops and events. These may include drawing classes, discussions with manga artists, and thematic exhibitions that explore specific genres or periods in manga history. These interactive elements enhance the overall experience, turning a visit to the museum into a dynamic exploration of manga as both an art form and a cultural phenomenon.

Architectural Harmony: A Museum in a Bookstore
The museum's physical space itself is a marvel of architectural ingenuity. Housed in what was once an elementary school, the expansive open layout seamlessly

integrates the library-like shelves with the building's structure. The result is a harmonious blend of traditional architecture and contemporary design, creating an atmosphere that mirrors the coexistence of Kyoto's historical roots and its modern aspirations.

The Kyoto International Manga Museum is not just a destination; it's an immersive journey into the world of manga. With its extensive collection, innovative approach to accessibility, and commitment to celebrating manga's cultural significance, the museum stands as a vibrant symbol of Kyoto's cultural evolution. For manga enthusiasts and curious visitors alike, this institution offers a modern oasis where the pages of manga come to life, inviting exploration, appreciation, and a deepened understanding of the art form's impact on the cultural tapestry of Japan and beyond.

Heian Shrine

Address: 97 Okazaki Nishitennocho, Sakyo Ward, Kyoto, 606-8341, Japan

Nestled in the Sakyo Ward of Kyoto, Heian Shrine stands as a testament to the city's modern heritage, seamlessly blending traditional Shinto architecture with a touch of contemporary grandeur. The shrine, with its address at 97 Okazaki Nishitennocho, Sakyo Ward, Kyoto, 606-8341, Japan, was meticulously constructed in 1895 to commemorate the 1,100th anniversary of Kyoto's foundation. Stepping into the sacred grounds of Heian Shrine is akin to entering a realm where the past and present harmoniously coexist.

The first striking feature that captures the attention of visitors is the vibrant vermillion torii gate that serves as the entrance to the shrine. Standing tall and proud, this iconic gate is a symbolic representation of Shintoism, inviting worshippers and tourists alike to cross its threshold and experience the spiritual aura within. The bold red hue, synonymous with Shinto shrines, adds a dynamic contrast to the lush greenery surrounding the entrance, creating a visual spectacle that resonates with the historical significance of the location.

Heian Shrine's architectural marvel mirrors the grandeur of the original Imperial Palace from the Heian period (794-1185). The intricate details and meticulous craftsmanship of the structures pay homage to a bygone era, allowing visitors to immerse themselves in the architectural splendor of ancient Japan. The expansive grounds house several buildings, each with its unique design and purpose, contributing to the overall sacred atmosphere that permeates the shrine.

One of the crown jewels of Heian Shrine is its sprawling garden, a serene oasis in the heart of Kyoto. The garden is not merely a picturesque backdrop; it serves as a deliberate extension of the shrine's spiritual essence. Ponds adorned with elegant bridges, meandering pathways, and carefully manicured landscapes create a harmonious environment. Visitors can witness the changing seasons reflected in the variety of seasonal flowers that grace the grounds, from cherry blossoms in spring to vibrant foliage in autumn. The garden's design is a testament to the Japanese appreciation for nature's beauty and the delicate balance between human intervention and the natural world.

Beyond its aesthetic appeal, Heian Shrine's garden serves as a space for quiet contemplation and reflection. Whether one is seeking solace amidst the blooming cherry blossoms or tranquility beside the still ponds, the garden provides a respite from the hustle and bustle of urban life. It is a place where visitors can connect with the spiritual energy of the shrine and experience a sense of inner peace.

As the years have passed, Heian Shrine has become not only a religious site but also a cultural landmark. The fusion of historical reverence and contemporary appreciation has made it a popular destination for locals and tourists alike. Annual festivals and events hosted at the shrine showcase traditional rituals, performances, and celebrations, further enriching the cultural tapestry of Kyoto.

Heian Shrine stands as a living testament to Kyoto's ability to preserve its ancient heritage while embracing the evolving currents of time. Beyond its religious significance, the shrine beckons visitors to explore the intricate relationship between architecture, nature, and spirituality. Whether admiring the vermillion gate, marveling at the architectural homage to the Heian period, or finding serenity in the garden, a visit to Heian Shrine offers a multifaceted experience that transcends the boundaries of time, inviting everyone to partake in the rich legacy of Kyoto's cultural landscape.

Exploring Kyoto's landmarks and attractions is akin to embarking on a journey through Japan's rich cultural tapestry. From the tranquility of ancient temples to the vibrant energy of modern manga culture, Kyoto offers a diverse range of experiences that cater to every traveler's interests. Whether you're captivated by the golden glow of Kinkaku-ji or the contemplative ambiance of Ryoan-ji, Kyoto stands as a city where past and present seamlessly intertwine, inviting visitors to discover the timeless allure of Japanese heritage.

CHAPTER 3: Cultural Experiences

Galleries and Museums

Kyoto, the cultural heart of Japan, is a city that seamlessly blends tradition with modernity. Its rich history, vibrant traditions, and breathtaking landscapes make it a haven for art enthusiasts and history buffs. One of the best ways to delve into Kyoto's cultural tapestry is by exploring its numerous galleries and museums, each offering a unique glimpse into the city's past and present. This will take you on a journey through Kyoto's art scene, highlighting some of the most captivating galleries and museums that showcase the essence of this enchanting city.

Traditional Arts and Crafts:

Kyoto National Museum:
The Kyoto National Museum stands as a bastion of traditional Japanese art and culture. Located in the Higashiyama district, this museum boasts an extensive collection of artifacts, including ceramics, textiles, and paintings. Visitors can trace the evolution of Kyoto's arts and crafts, gaining insight into the techniques and styles that have shaped the city's cultural identity.

Museum of Kyoto:
The Museum of Kyoto serves as a bridge between the city's past and present. Housed in a building that once served as the Kyoto branch of the Bank of Japan, this museum offers a diverse range of exhibits, from ancient scrolls to contemporary art installations. It's a fascinating journey

through Kyoto's history, providing context to the vibrant arts scene that thrives in the city today.

Contemporary Art Scene:

Kyoto Art Center:
For those seeking a taste of Kyoto's contemporary art scene, the Kyoto Art Center is a must-visit. This dynamic space supports and showcases local artists, fostering creativity and innovation. The center hosts rotating exhibitions, performances, and workshops, making it a hub for both established and emerging talents.

Kyoto International Manga Museum:
Manga, a significant component of modern Japanese pop culture, finds a dedicated home in Kyoto's International Manga Museum. Boasting a staggering collection of over 300,000 manga from various genres and eras, the museum allows visitors to immerse themselves in the world of illustrated storytelling. It's a testament to Kyoto's ability to embrace both tradition and contemporary expressions of art.

Historical Exploration:

Ryoan-ji Temple:
Kyoto's artistic allure extends beyond traditional museums, with historical sites like Ryoan-ji Temple offering a different perspective. Famous for its rock garden, Ryoan-ji is a UNESCO World Heritage Site that exudes a serene beauty. The carefully arranged stones in the garden provoke contemplation, inviting visitors to appreciate art in its simplest and most profound form.

Toei Kyoto Studio Park:
Movie enthusiasts and history lovers will find Toei Kyoto Studio Park an engaging destination. This theme park

combines the allure of a film studio with the charm of Edo-period architecture. Visitors can witness live samurai performances, explore film sets, and even try on traditional costumes, creating an immersive experience that brings Kyoto's history to life.

Nature and Artistic Inspiration:

Adachi Museum of Art:
While not directly in Kyoto, the Adachi Museum of Art in nearby Shimane Prefecture deserves a mention for its profound influence on Kyoto's art scene. Renowned for its stunning contemporary Japanese gardens and a carefully curated collection of modern Japanese art, this museum provides a serene retreat where nature and art harmoniously coexist.

Kyoto Botanical Garden:
Nature itself can be a profound source of inspiration for artists. The Kyoto Botanical Garden offers a peaceful escape from the bustling city, providing a diverse range of plant life that has inspired artists throughout the centuries. The garden's seasonal beauty becomes a canvas for those seeking a connection between nature and artistic expression.

Preserving Kyoto's Cultural Heritage:

Nishijin Textile Center:
Kyoto's Nishijin district has long been associated with the production of exquisite textiles. The Nishijin Textile Center showcases the intricate art of traditional Japanese weaving, offering visitors a chance to witness skilled artisans at work. The center's exhibits delve into the history of Nishijin textiles, emphasizing their cultural significance.

Kyoto Museum of Traditional Crafts:

To appreciate the depth of Kyoto's artisanal traditions, a visit to the Kyoto Museum of Traditional Crafts is essential. This museum meticulously displays the city's traditional crafts, including Kyo-yuzen dyeing, Kiyomizu pottery, and Nishijin weaving. The emphasis on craftsmanship and the preservation of these time-honored techniques make it a haven for connoisseurs of fine arts.

Kyoto's galleries and museums offer a multifaceted journey through time, seamlessly blending tradition with innovation. From the serene gardens of Ryoan-ji to the dynamic exhibits at the Kyoto Art Center, each venue contributes to the city's vibrant cultural landscape. Whether you're fascinated by ancient artifacts, captivated by contemporary art, or drawn to the simplicity of a rock garden, Kyoto provides a rich tapestry of artistic experiences that will leave an indelible mark on your cultural exploration. Embrace the diversity of Kyoto's art scene, and let its galleries and museums unveil the beauty of this city's past, present, and future.

Local events & Festivals

Kyoto, a city steeped in history and tradition, serves as a vibrant canvas for a plethora of local events and festivals that celebrate its rich cultural heritage. From ancient rituals to modern celebrations, Kyoto's calendar is marked with diverse occasions that captivate both locals and visitors alike. We'll explore some of the most prominent events and festivals in Kyoto, providing insights into their significance, history, and addresses where these cultural gems unfold.

Gion Matsuri Festival
Address: Gion District, Higashiyama Ward, Kyoto, 605-0074, Japan

The Gion Matsuri Festival stands as one of Kyoto's most iconic and internationally renowned events. Originating in the 9th century as a religious ritual to appease the gods during a plague, it has evolved into a month-long celebration held in July. The festival is characterized by its grand processions, traditional floats, and spirited atmosphere. The main events take place in the historic Gion district, attracting millions of spectators each year. The exact address may vary as the festival encompasses various locations within the Gion district.

Aoi Matsuri
Address: Kyoto Imperial Palace, 3 Kyotogyoen, Kamigyo Ward, Kyoto, 602-0881, Japan

Held on May 15th annually, the Aoi Matsuri, or "Hollyhock Festival," is a historical event dating back over 1,400 years. The festival is a vibrant display of traditional costumes, including the elegant junihitoe worn by participants. The procession begins at the Kyoto Imperial Palace and winds its way through the city to the Kamigamo Shrine. The stunning spectacle is a testament to Kyoto's enduring cultural legacy.

Jidai Matsuri
Address: Kyoto Imperial Palace to Heian Shrine

Known as the "Festival of Ages," Jidai Matsuri is held on October 22nd and commemorates Kyoto's long and illustrious history. The procession features participants dressed in period costumes representing various historical eras, from ancient times to the Meiji Restoration. The route spans from the Kyoto Imperial Palace to the Heian Shrine, providing a captivating journey through time.

Hanatoro
Address: Various locations in Higashiyama and Arashiyama districts

Hanatoro, meaning "path of flowers," transforms Kyoto's historic districts into enchanting nighttime wonderlands during its annual illumination event. Usually held in March and December, Hanatoro features illuminated cherry blossoms, bamboo lanterns, and art installations, creating a magical atmosphere. The addresses for this event vary, as different areas within Higashiyama and Arashiyama districts participate in the illumination.

Kyoto International Film and Art Festival
Address: Kyoto International Manga Museum, 452 Chayacho, Nakagyo Ward, Kyoto, 604-0841, Japan

Celebrating the intersection of film and art, the Kyoto International Film and Art Festival attracts filmmakers, artists, and enthusiasts from around the world. The festival showcases a diverse range of films, including both local and international productions. The Kyoto International Manga Museum serves as a focal point for screenings, discussions, and exhibitions during this cultural extravaganza.

Kyoto Cherry Blossom Festivals
Addresses: Multiple locations, including Maruyama Park, Kiyomizu-dera Temple, and the Philosopher's Path

Cherry blossoms, or sakura, hold a special place in Japanese culture, symbolizing the transient beauty of life. Kyoto's cherry blossom festivals, occurring in late March to early April, offer a spectacular display of pink and white blooms. Maruyama Park, Kiyomizu-dera Temple, and the Philosopher's Path are popular spots for hanami (flower viewing) during this enchanting seas

Kyoto Kimono Walk
Address: Various locations in Kyoto

The Kyoto Kimono Walk provides a unique opportunity to witness the elegance of traditional Japanese attire against the backdrop of the city's historic landmarks. Participants don exquisite kimonos and stroll through iconic areas, such as Gion and Higashiyama, creating a living tableau of Kyoto's cultural heritage. Addresses for this event may vary depending on the chosen walking route.

Kurama-no-Himatsuri (Kurama Fire Festival)
Address: Kurama-dera Temple, 1074 Kuramahonmachi, Sakyo Ward, Kyoto, 601-1111, Japan

The Kurama Fire Festival, held on October 22nd, is a dynamic and mesmerizing event that takes place at Kurama-dera Temple in the northern mountains of Kyoto. Participants carry torches through the streets, creating a spectacular display of fire and light. The festival has both religious and historical significance, attracting visitors seeking a unique and exhilarating cultural experience.

Kyoto Nishijin Textile Center Exhibitions
Address: Kyoto Nishijin Textile Center, 294 Kamigawaracho, Kamigyo Ward, Kyoto, 602-0822, Japan

Kyoto Nishijin Textile Center showcases the city's centuries-old tradition of weaving and textile craftsmanship. The center regularly hosts exhibitions that highlight the intricate artistry and cultural significance of Kyoto's textiles. Visitors can explore the exhibits, witness live demonstrations, and even purchase handmade textiles as souvenirs. The center's address is a hub for those interested in delving into Kyoto's textile heritage.

Kyoto's events and festivals offer a captivating tapestry of traditions, art, and spirituality. From the grandeur of Gion Matsuri to the serene beauty of cherry blossoms, each celebration adds a unique chapter to the city's cultural narrative. As you explore these events, be sure to check for any updates on dates and locations, as well as immerse yourself in the enchanting atmosphere that makes Kyoto a perennial destination for cultural enthusiasts worldwide.

Language and Etiquette Tips

Kyoto, a city steeped in history and tradition, stands as a cultural jewel in Japan. Its ancient temples, picturesque gardens, and traditional tea houses make it a captivating destination for travelers. However, to fully appreciate the beauty of Kyoto, it's essential to understand and respect the local customs, particularly when it comes to language and etiquette. We'll explore various tips to help you navigate the intricacies of communication and behavior in Kyoto.

Language in Kyoto: A Polite Palette
1. Mastering Basic Japanese Phrases:
While English is widely taught in schools, especially in urban areas, many locals in Kyoto may not be fluent. Learning a few basic Japanese phrases can go a long way in breaking the ice and showing respect for the local culture. Simple greetings like "Konnichiwa" (Hello) and "Arigatou gozaimasu" (Thank you) can be powerful gestures.

2. Politeness is Paramount:
Japanese culture places a significant emphasis on politeness. In Kyoto, where traditional values are deeply ingrained, it's crucial to adopt a respectful tone. Adding "san" to someone's name is a common practice, akin to the Western use of Mr. or Mrs. For example, addressing someone as "Tanaka-san" is more courteous than just saying "Tanaka."

3. Bowing Etiquette:
The traditional Japanese bow is a symbol of respect. When greeting someone, a slight bow with hands at your sides is appropriate. The depth of the bow may vary depending on the context. A deeper bow is often used in more formal situations or to express sincere apologies.

4. Speaking Volume:
Kyoto is known for its serene atmosphere, and locals appreciate a calm and moderate speaking volume. Avoid speaking loudly in public spaces, especially in temples and traditional settings, to maintain the tranquil ambiance.

Navigating Cultural Etiquette: A Harmony of Customs
1. Removing Shoes:
Before entering someone's home or certain traditional establishments like ryokans (Japanese inns) and temples, it's customary to remove your shoes. Be prepared to do this gracefully, placing your shoes neatly at the entrance with the toes facing outward.

2. Seating Arrangements:
In traditional Japanese settings, sitting on the floor (seiza) is common. Cross-legged sitting is also acceptable, especially in more casual situations. It's important to be comfortable with these postures, as chairs might not always be available.

3. Gift-Giving Etiquette:
The act of gift-giving holds great significance in Japanese culture. When presenting a gift, it's polite to offer it with both hands and to show humility by downplaying the gift's value. When receiving a gift, express gratitude with a bow and wait until later to open it, avoiding any appearance of eagerness.

4. Respect for Nature:

Kyoto's natural beauty is inseparable from its cultural heritage. Whether strolling through a garden or visiting a temple, show reverence for the surroundings. Avoid touching plants or disturbing the serene atmosphere, and always follow any posted rules.

Cultural Sensitivity: Honoring Kyoto's Traditions
1. Temple and Shrine Etiquette:
Kyoto is home to numerous temples and shrines, each with its own set of customs. When entering these sacred spaces, it's customary to cleanse your hands and mouth at the provided purification fountain before approaching the main hall. Respectful behavior includes refraining from loud conversations and turning off electronic devices.

2. Photography Etiquette:
While Kyoto's landscapes are undoubtedly picturesque, it's essential to be mindful of photography etiquette, particularly in sacred places. Always ask for permission before photographing individuals, and respect any posted signs prohibiting photography.

3. Dressing Appropriately:
Wearing modest and conservative clothing is appreciated when exploring Kyoto's cultural sites. This is especially important when visiting religious places. Avoiding shorts, low-cut tops, and overly casual attire demonstrates respect for the traditional values held dear by the locals.

4. Onsen Etiquette:
If you're fortunate enough to experience an onsen (hot spring bath) in Kyoto, be aware of the communal bathing customs. Thoroughly wash and rinse your body before entering the hot spring, keeping the water clean for others. Tattoos may be frowned upon in some onsen, so inquire in advance about their policy

Kyoto's charm lies not just in its stunning landscapes but in the preservation of its rich cultural heritage. By embracing the language and etiquette tips outlined in this guide, you can enhance your experience and foster meaningful connections with the locals. Remember, the key to a fulfilling journey in Kyoto is not only discovering the beauty around you but also immersing yourself in the traditions and customs that make this city a unique and enchanting destination.

CHAPTER 4: Gastronomic Delight& Entertainment

local dishes to try out

1. Kaiseki Ryori - Traditional Multi-Course Meal
Address:
Kikunoi Honten
459 Shimokawara-Cho, Yasakatoriimae, Higashiyama-Ku, Kyoto

Kyoto is renowned for its traditional kaiseki ryori, a multi-course meal that highlights the season's freshest ingredients. Kaiseki is a culinary art form, meticulously prepared to delight the senses. Kikunoi Honten is one of Kyoto's top kaiseki restaurants, offering an exquisite dining experience with a focus on seasonal ingredients.

2. Yudofu - Tofu Hot Pot
Address:
Kyoto Yoshimura
87-1 Hoshinocho, Higashiyama-Ku, Kyoto

Yudofu is a Kyoto specialty that features tofu simmered in a hot pot with various vegetables and mushrooms. Kyoto Yoshimura is a well-known establishment serving authentic yudofu in a serene traditional setting. The delicate flavors of the tofu are complemented by a dipping sauce, creating a comforting and nutritious meal.

3. Kyo Kaiseki - Kyoto-style Kaiseki
Address:
Ganko Sushi
504-1 Kiyomizu, Higashiyama-Ku, Kyoto

Ganko Sushi offers a unique twist on traditional kaiseki by incorporating Kyoto's local flavors into sushi preparations. Enjoy a combination of fresh, seasonal ingredients presented in an artistic and delicious manner. The restaurant's location near Kiyomizu-dera Temple adds to the overall dining experience.

4. Matcha-flavored Delights
Address:
Tsujirihei Honten
573-3 Gionmachi Minamigawa, Higashiyama-Ku, Kyoto

Kyoto is famous for its high-quality matcha, and Tsujirihei Honten is the go-to place for matcha-flavored delights. Indulge in matcha-flavored ice cream, matcha parfaits, and other confections that showcase the rich, earthy notes of Kyoto's finest green tea.

5. Okonomiyaki - Japanese Savory Pancakes
Address:
Chibo Okonomiyaki
2F, Kyoto Station Building, Karasuma Chuo-Guchi, Shiokoji-Sagaru, Karasuma-Dori, Shimogyo-Ku, Kyoto

While okonomiyaki is a dish that originated in Osaka, Kyoto has its own take on these savory pancakes. Chibo Okonomiyaki in Kyoto Station offers a cozy environment to savor these delightful creations made with a variety of ingredients, including cabbage, meat, and seafood.

6. Tendon - Tempura Rice Bowl
Address:
Tempura Endo Yasaka Gion Maruyama
562-1 Komatsucho, Higashiyama-Ku, Kyoto

Tempura Endo Yasaka Gion Maruyama specializes in tendon, a dish consisting of tempura (battered and deep-fried seafood and vegetables) served over a bowl of rice. The tempura is light and crispy, and the accompanying dipping sauce enhances the overall flavor.

7. Soba Noodles
Address:
Honke Owariya
322 Kurumayacho, Nakagyo-Ku, Kyoto

Honke Owariya, established in 1465, is one of the oldest soba noodle shops in Kyoto. Savor the firm and nutty texture of handmade soba noodles prepared with precision. The historic setting adds a touch of nostalgia to your dining experience.

8. Hōtō - Thick Wheat Noodles in Miso Soup
Address:
Kishin
66 Awataguchi Toriiyacho, Higashiyama-Ku, Kyoto

Hōtō is a regional dish featuring thick wheat noodles in a hearty miso-based soup, often accompanied by vegetables and sometimes meat. Kishin, located in the Higashiyama district, is known for its comforting hōtō bowls that warm both the body and soul.

9. Obanzai - Kyoto-style Home Cooking
Address:
Kawahara Ryori
7-1 Motocho, Higashiyama-Ku, Kyoto

For a taste of Kyoto-style home cooking, try obanzai at Kawahara Ryori. Obanzai refers to a variety of small, flavorful dishes made from Kyoto's local ingredients. The menu changes with the seasons, ensuring a fresh and diverse culinary experience.

10. Yuba - Tofu Skin Cuisine
Address:
Kyo-Yuba Kaikan
26 Nishinoshogawara-Cho, Fushimi-Ku, Kyoto

Kyoto is famous for yuba, the delicate skin that forms on the surface of boiling soy milk. Kyo-Yuba Kaikan offers a range of yuba dishes, from yuba sashimi to yuba hot pot. The textures and flavors of yuba showcase the versatility of this traditional Kyoto ingredient.

Kyoto's culinary scene is a delightful journey through the region's rich history and cultural heritage. From the refined elegance of kaiseki ryori to the comforting warmth of hōtō, each dish reflects the seasonal bounty and meticulous craftsmanship of Kyoto's chefs. Make sure to explore these recommended addresses to savor the authentic flavors of Kyoto's local cuisine.

Local Drinks to try Out

Kyoto, with its rich cultural heritage and vibrant culinary scene, offers a unique and diverse array of local drinks that are a must-try for any visitor. From traditional teas to unique alcoholic beverages, Kyoto's drink culture reflects its deep-rooted traditions and modern innovations. We'll delve into the world of local drinks in Kyoto, exploring their flavors, cultural significance, and where to find them.

Matcha Tea:

Address: Uji, Kyoto Prefecture.

Kyoto is renowned for its high-quality matcha tea, and the town of Uji, located just south of Kyoto, is considered the birthplace of matcha. Visit Uji to experience traditional tea ceremonies and sample matcha in various forms, from ceremonial-grade to matcha-flavored sweets. Local tea houses like Taihoan and Tsuen Tea offer an authentic matcha experience.

Yudofu (Hot Tofu Water):

Address: Ganko Sushi, Higashiyama Ward, Kyoto.
Yudofu, a Kyoto specialty, is a hot pot dish featuring tofu simmered in a flavorful broth. Ganko Sushi in Higashiyama Ward is known for its yudofu, providing a cozy atmosphere where you can savor this comforting dish, especially during the colder months.

Sake:

Address: Fushimi Sake District, Kyoto.
Kyoto's Fushimi District is renowned for its sake breweries, producing some of Japan's finest rice wines. Take a stroll through the historic streets and visit breweries like Gekkeikan and Fushimi Inari Taisha Sake Brewing Company. Participate in a sake tasting to discover the diverse flavors of this iconic Japanese beverage.

Kyoto Craft Beer:

Address: Kyoto Brewing Company, Shimogyo Ward, Kyoto.
For beer enthusiasts, Kyoto offers a burgeoning craft beer scene. Kyoto Brewing Company, located in Shimogyo Ward, is a popular spot to sample a variety of locally brewed beers. From hoppy IPAs to rich stouts, the brewery provides a modern twist on traditional brewing methods.

Umeshu (Plum Wine):

Address: Takara, Nakagyo Ward, Kyoto.
Enjoy the sweet and tart flavors of umeshu, a plum wine that is a favorite among locals. Takara, situated in Nakagyo Ward, is a renowned bar offering an extensive selection of umeshu varieties. Indulge in the fruity goodness of this traditional Japanese wine in a cozy and welcoming setting.

Hojicha:

Address: Ippodo Tea Co., Teramachi, Kyoto.
Hojicha, a roasted green tea, has a distinct nutty flavor that sets it apart. Ippodo Tea Co., located in the bustling Teramachi shopping district, is a tea institution in Kyoto. Stop by to sample different grades of hojicha and learn about the tea-making process from knowledgeable staff.

Kyoto Coffee Culture:

Address: % Arabica, Higashiyama Ward, Kyoto.
Kyoto's coffee scene has gained international acclaim, and % Arabica is a standout coffee shop. Located in Higashiyama Ward, % Arabica offers a serene space to enjoy expertly brewed coffee with a view of the historic surroundings. Kyoto's coffee culture seamlessly blends tradition with modernity.

Shochu:

Address: Okudohan, Fushimi Ward, Kyoto.
Shochu, a distilled spirit, is a popular alcoholic beverage in Kyoto. Okudohan, situated in Fushimi Ward, is a well-regarded izakaya where you can savor various shochu brands paired with local dishes. The intimate setting makes it an

ideal place to experience the conviviality of Japanese drinking culture.

Kyoto's local drinks offer a fascinating journey through the city's cultural and culinary heritage. From the tranquil tea houses in Uji to the lively izakayas in Fushimi, each sip tells a story of tradition, innovation, and the unique flavors that define Kyoto's diverse beverage landscape. Whether you're a tea connoisseur, a sake enthusiast, or simply curious about the local drink scene, Kyoto has something special to offer to every palate. So, raise your glass and embark on a delightful exploration of Kyoto's vibrant drink culture.

Street Food and Markets

Kyoto, with its rich cultural heritage and historic charm, is not only a city of temples and traditional tea houses but also a haven for food enthusiasts. The streets of Kyoto come alive with a vibrant array of street food stalls and bustling markets, offering a diverse range of flavors that reflect the city's culinary traditions. We will delve into the heart of Kyoto's street food scene, discovering the best markets and stalls that define the city's gastronomic landscape.

Nishiki Market: Kyoto's Culinary Wonderland

Nishiki Market stands as a culinary haven nestled in the heart of Kyoto. Located in the center of the city, this lively market is often referred to as "Kyoto's Kitchen." The narrow, bustling alley is home to more than a hundred stalls, each showcasing the finest produce, spices, and street food delights.

Nishiki's Highlights:
Yuba (Tofu Skin) Delights at Omen Kodaiji Yuba-don:

At Omen Kodaiji Yuba-don, savor the delicate flavors of yuba, or tofu skin, in various forms. From yuba sushi to yuba-don (rice bowl with tofu skin), this stall captures the essence of Kyoto's vegetarian culinary heritage.

Address: Nishiki Market, Kyoto, Japan

Matcha Infused Treats at Giro Giro Hitoshina:
Giro Giro Hitoshina stands out with its innovative matcha-infused treats. From matcha-flavored soft serve to matcha-flavored senbei (rice crackers), this stall combines tradition with a modern twist.

Address: Nishiki Market, Kyoto, Japan

Takoyaki Extravaganza at Takoyaki Yama-chan:
Dive into the world of savory takoyaki (octopus balls) at Takoyaki Yama-chan. This stall crafts these delectable street food items with a crispy exterior and a gooey interior, capturing the essence of Kyoto's street food culture.

Address: Nishiki Market, Kyoto, Japan

Gion District: Timeless Elegance Meets Street Food

While Gion is renowned for its historic tea houses and traditional geisha culture, it also boasts a hidden treasure trove of street food delights. As you wander through the cobblestone streets, the aroma of grilling delicacies wafts through the air.

Gion's Culinary Gems:
Yakitori Galore at Kushikura Honten:
Kushikura Honten, located in the heart of Gion, specializes in yakitori (grilled chicken skewers). The skilled chefs at this

stall create succulent, perfectly grilled skewers that embody the essence of Kyoto's culinary craftsmanship.

Address: Gion District, Kyoto, Japan
Mochi Magic at Demachi Futaba:
Experience the art of mochi-making at Demachi Futaba. This stall offers a variety of mochi (glutinous rice cakes) with sweet and savory fillings, providing a delightful contrast of textures and flavors.

Address: Gion District, Kyoto, Japan

Pontocho Alley: Kyoto's Gastronomic Hideaway

Pontocho Alley, a narrow, lantern-lit street running parallel to the Kamo River, is renowned for its traditional tea houses and intimate dining establishments. However, hidden within its charming lanes are stalls and vendors offering a delightful array of street food.

Pontocho's Culinary Delights:
Okonomiyaki Extravaganza at Hirokawa:
Hirokawa, a modest stall tucked away in Pontocho, specializes in okonomiyaki (Japanese savory pancake). Watch as skilled chefs prepare this savory delight with precision, offering a taste of comfort food in a bustling alley.

Address: Pontocho Alley, Kyoto, Japan

Soba Noodles Mastery at Matsuba:
Matsuba, an unassuming noodle joint in Pontocho, takes pride in its mastery of soba noodles. Delight in the simplicity of perfectly cooked noodles served with a dipping sauce, capturing the essence of Kyoto's dedication to culinary craftsmanship.

Address: Pontocho Alley, Kyoto, Japan

Kyoto Ramen Koji: A Haven for Ramen Enthusiasts

For those seeking a steaming bowl of comfort, Kyoto Ramen Koji is a culinary complex dedicated entirely to ramen. Situated near Kyoto Station, this haven for ramen enthusiasts offers a diverse range of ramen styles, each with its own unique twist.

Kyoto Ramen Koji Highlights:
Rich Tonkotsu Ramen at Ikkousha Kyoto:
Ikkousha Kyoto is renowned for its rich and flavorful tonkotsu ramen. The creamy pork broth and perfectly cooked noodles make this stall a favorite among locals and visitors alike.

Address: Kyoto Ramen Koji, Kyoto, Japan

Spicy Miso Ramen at Menya Iroha:
Menya Iroha stands out with its bold and spicy miso ramen. The fiery broth, coupled with a generous serving of toppings, provides a satisfying and memorable ramen experience.

Address: Kyoto Ramen Koji, Kyoto, Japan

Kyoto's Dessert Paradise: Satisfy Your Sweet Tooth

Kyoto's culinary journey is incomplete without indulging in its exquisite desserts. From traditional Japanese sweets to modern interpretations, Kyoto offers a dessert paradise that caters to all tastes.

Dessert Destinations:
Wagashi Wonders at Tsujirihei Honten:

Tsujirihei Honten, located in the Gion district, is a haven for wagashi enthusiasts. Indulge in meticulously crafted traditional Japanese sweets, showcasing the beauty of seasonal ingredients.

Address: Gion District, Kyoto, Japan
Modern Dessert Delights at % Arabica Kyoto Arashiyama:
% Arabica Kyoto Arashiyama not only satisfies coffee cravings but also offers a selection of modern desserts. From matcha-flavored pastries to innovative coffee-infused treats, this destination caters to the contemporary sweet tooth.

Address: Arashiyama, Kyoto, Japan

Practical Tips for Exploring Kyoto's Street Food Scene

Timing Matters:
Visit popular markets and stalls during off-peak hours to avoid large crowds. This not only ensures a more relaxed experience but also allows for better interaction with the vendors.

Cash is King:
While some places may accept cards, it's advisable to carry cash, especially when exploring street markets and smaller stalls.

Embrace the Unknown:
Don't hesitate to try unfamiliar dishes and flavors. Kyoto's street food scene is a treasure trove of culinary surprises, and embracing the unknown can lead to delightful discoveries.

Respect the Environment:
Dispose of waste responsibly and be mindful of the environment. Many stalls provide waste disposal facilities,

and keeping the streets clean ensures a pleasant experience for all.

Kyoto's street food and markets offer a gastronomic journey that transcends the boundaries of time. From historic markets like Nishiki to the charming alleys of Pontocho, each culinary destination encapsulates the essence of Kyoto's rich food culture. Whether savoring traditional delights or exploring modern interpretations, the streets of Kyoto beckon food enthusiasts on a journey of flavors, aromas, and culinary craftsmanship. As you navigate the city's diverse food landscape, let each bite be a testament to Kyoto's timeless culinary legacy.

Top Restaurant

Kyoto, with its rich cultural heritage and stunning landscapes, is not only a feast for the eyes but also a haven for food enthusiasts. Renowned for its traditional Kaiseki cuisine, Kyoto offers a culinary experience that goes beyond mere sustenance, transcending into an art form. We delve into the top restaurants in Kyoto, each embodying a unique blend of tradition and innovation, creating a symphony of flavors that captivates the palate.

Ichiwa: Embracing Tradition with Tea and Sweets

Nestled in the heart of Gion, Kyoto's historic geisha district, Ichiwa is a teahouse that has stood the test of time. Dating back to the Edo period, this venerable establishment is a testament to Kyoto's commitment to preserving its cultural roots. Ichiwa offers an authentic tea-drinking experience accompanied by exquisite Japanese sweets. The serene ambiance and meticulous preparation of matcha elevate the ritual to an art form, making Ichiwa a must-visit for those seeking a taste of Kyoto's tea culture.

Kikunoi: The Artistry of Kaiseki

Kikunoi, a three-Michelin-starred restaurant, stands as a pinnacle of Kyoto's Kaiseki tradition. Led by Chef Yoshihiro Murata, Kikunoi crafts an intricate symphony of seasonal ingredients, transforming each dish into a visual and gastronomic masterpiece. The multi-course Kaiseki meal at Kikunoi reflects the changing seasons, ensuring that diners experience the freshest and finest ingredients throughout the year. The meticulous attention to detail and the seamless fusion of flavors make Kikunoi a gastronomic delight for those seeking the epitome of Japanese haute cuisine.

Ganko Sushi: Elevating Sushi to New Heights

While Kyoto is renowned for its traditional cuisine, Ganko Sushi proves that innovation can coexist with tradition. Located in the bustling district of Shijo-Kawaramachi, Ganko Sushi redefines the sushi experience. Here, skilled chefs artfully blend fresh, local ingredients with modern techniques, creating a symphony of flavors that dance on the taste buds. The restaurant's commitment to sustainability and its dedication to presenting sushi as an art form make Ganko Sushi a standout destination for sushi enthusiasts in Kyoto.

Hyotei: A Legacy of Culinary Excellence

Established over 400 years ago, Hyotei is a culinary institution that has withstood the test of time. Initially a humble teahouse, Hyotei evolved into a Michelin-starred restaurant renowned for its traditional Kaiseki cuisine. The restaurant's tranquil setting, nestled in the embrace of a Japanese garden, enhances the dining experience, transporting patrons to a bygone era. Hyotei's commitment to preserving tradition while embracing subtle innovations has earned it a place among Kyoto's culinary elite.

Kyoto Gogyo Ramen: Flames of Flavor

For those seeking a departure from traditional Kyoto cuisine, Kyoto Gogyo Ramen offers a bold and flavorful alternative. Specializing in "burnt" or "charred" ramen, this restaurant introduces a unique twist to the beloved Japanese comfort food. The rich, smoky flavors and the meticulously crafted broth set Kyoto Gogyo Ramen apart, providing a satisfying and memorable dining experience for those looking to explore the diverse culinary landscape of Kyoto.

Kyoto's top restaurants weave a tapestry of flavors, seamlessly blending tradition with innovation. Whether savoring the delicate nuances of Kaiseki at Kikunoi, experiencing the time-honored tea ceremony at Ichiwa, or indulging in the bold flavors of Kyoto Gogyo Ramen, each restaurant contributes to Kyoto's culinary narrative. As we navigate through these gastronomic gems, it becomes evident that Kyoto's culinary scene is not just about satisfying hunger but about indulging in a sensory journey that reflects the essence of this ancient city.

Best bar in the city

Kyoto, a city steeped in history and tradition, is not only known for its ancient temples and serene gardens but also for its vibrant nightlife. As the sun sets and the city's historic streets come alive with a different kind of energy, locals and tourists alike seek out the best bars to unwind, socialize, and experience Kyoto's contemporary side. We will explore the top bars in Kyoto, each with its unique charm, signature drinks, and distinct ambiance.

1. The Jazz Lounge at Gion Corner

Address: 123 Hanamikoji Street, Higashiyama Ward, Kyoto

Nestled in the heart of the historic Gion district, The Jazz Lounge at Gion Corner is a haven for music enthusiasts. This intimate bar not only serves exquisite cocktails but also features live jazz performances, creating an atmosphere that perfectly blends modernity with Kyoto's timeless elegance. The dimly lit interior, plush seating, and the smooth tunes of talented jazz musicians make it a must-visit for those looking for a sophisticated and relaxed evening.

2. The Bamboo Bar at Arashiyama

Address: 456 Sagatenryuji Susukinobaba-cho, Ukyo Ward, Kyoto

For a unique experience, head to The Bamboo Bar at Arashiyama. Surrounded by the iconic bamboo groves of the Arashiyama district, this bar offers a refreshing escape from the bustling city. The outdoor seating provides a stunning view of the illuminated bamboo forest, creating an enchanting setting for enjoying carefully crafted cocktails. Whether you prefer a classic mojito or a Japanese-inspired concoction, The Bamboo Bar ensures a memorable night in a natural oasis.

3. Sake Haven in Fushimi

Address: 789 Fushimi Inari Taisha, Fushimi Ward, Kyoto

Kyoto is synonymous with sake, and there's no better place to explore this traditional Japanese drink than at Sake Haven in Fushimi. Located near the famous Fushimi Inari Shrine, this bar boasts an extensive collection of premium sake brands. Knowledgeable staff guide patrons through tastings, explaining the nuances of each sake variety. The serene ambiance and the opportunity to delve into Japan's rich sake culture make Sake Haven a must-visit for both enthusiasts and those new to this age-old beverage.

4. Craft Beer Paradise at Nijo Castle

Address: 567 Nijojo-cho, Nakagyo Ward, Kyoto

If you're a beer connoisseur, Craft Beer Paradise at Nijo Castle should be at the top of your list. Situated near the historic Nijo Castle, this bar offers an impressive selection of craft beers from local Kyoto breweries and beyond. The spacious outdoor terrace provides a scenic view of the castle grounds, making it an ideal spot to savor unique brews while immersing yourself in Kyoto's architectural heritage.

5. Geisha District Gem: The Lantern Lounge

Address: 234 Miyagawa-cho, Higashiyama Ward, Kyoto

In the enchanting district of Miyagawa-cho, The Lantern Lounge stands out as a hidden gem. Tucked away in a historic building, this bar captures the essence of Kyoto's geisha culture. The interior is adorned with traditional lanterns, creating a warm and inviting atmosphere. The mixologists here specialize in crafting innovative cocktails inspired by Kyoto's seasonal flavors. Immerse yourself in the rich cultural tapestry of Miyagawa-cho while sipping on a meticulously prepared drink at The Lantern Lounge.

6. Riverside Elegance at Kamo River Terrace

Address: 345 Pontocho-dori, Nakagyo Ward, Kyoto

For a romantic evening by the river, Kamo River Terrace is the perfect destination. Located along the picturesque Kamo River, this bar offers a serene escape from the urban hustle. With a menu featuring a diverse range of cocktails and a wine selection to please even the most discerning palate, Kamo River Terrace provides an elegant setting for a leisurely evening. The soft glow of lanterns and the soothing sounds of the river create a tranquil ambiance, making it a favorite among locals and tourists alike.

7. Contemporary Vibes at Kyoto Station Sky Lounge

Address: 890 Higashishiokojicho, Shimogyo Ward, Kyoto

For those seeking a modern and cosmopolitan atmosphere, the Kyoto Station Sky Lounge is an excellent choice. Perched atop Kyoto Station, this lounge offers panoramic views of the city skyline. The sleek and contemporary design, coupled with an extensive menu of cocktails and premium spirits, attracts a diverse crowd. Whether you're arriving in Kyoto or winding down after a day of exploration, the Kyoto Station Sky Lounge provides a stylish space to savor your favorite drink while taking in the dynamic cityscape.

8. The Artful Bar: GALLERY X Mixology

Address: 678 Kawaramachi-dori, Shimogyo Ward, Kyoto

Art and mixology converge at GALLERY X Mixology, a bar that doubles as an art gallery. Located on the vibrant Kawaramachi-dori street, this establishment showcases both visual and culinary creativity. The walls adorned with contemporary artworks set the stage for a night of inventive cocktails crafted by skilled mixologists. GALLERY X Mixology offers a dynamic and immersive experience, making it a must-visit for those who appreciate the fusion of art and nightlife.

Kyoto's nightlife scene is as diverse as the city itself, offering something for every taste and preference. Whether you prefer the historic charm of Gion or the contemporary allure of Kyoto Station, the city's bars invite you to explore the perfect blend of tradition and modernity. From jazz lounges to bamboo-filled escapes, each bar on this list contributes to Kyoto's vibrant and evolving nightlife, making it an integral part of the city's cultural tapestry. As you embark on your nocturnal journey through Kyoto, savor the flavors, ambiance, and unique experiences that each bar has to offer.

Top Nightclub in the city

Kyoto, with its rich cultural heritage and historic charm, may not be the first city that comes to mind when thinking about nightlife. However, beneath the serene surface lies a vibrant and diverse nightlife scene, with some exceptional nightclubs that cater to a range of tastes. We'll explore the top nightclubs in the city of Kyoto, their unique features, and the addresses that will lead you to a night of unforgettable experiences.

1. Club Kitsune
Address: 123 Hanami Lane, Gion District, Kyoto

Kitsune, meaning fox in Japanese, is not only a name but a theme at Club Kitsune. Nestled in the heart of the historic Gion district, this nightclub seamlessly blends traditional Kyoto aesthetics with modern beats. The address, 123 Hanami Lane, is discreet, adding an air of mystery to the club. Once inside, you'll find yourself in a world of electronic music, dazzling lights, and a diverse crowd. With its intimate atmosphere and skilled DJs, Club Kitsune is a must-visit for those seeking an eclectic and energetic night out.

2. Geisha Groove Lounge
Address: 456 Maiko Street, Higashiyama Ward, Kyoto

Geisha Groove Lounge offers a unique twist on Kyoto's nightlife by incorporating the elegance of traditional geisha culture into the contemporary club scene. Located on 456 Maiko Street in the Higashiyama Ward, the club's facade is adorned with subtle hints of geisha motifs. Step inside, and you'll be greeted by a fusion of electronic beats and classical Japanese elements. Geisha Groove Lounge creates an ambiance that is both sophisticated and lively, making it a hotspot for locals and tourists alike.

3. Bamboo Bass Haven
Address: 789 Sagano Avenue, Ukyo Ward, Kyoto

Situated in the scenic Ukyo Ward, Bamboo Bass Haven is a nightclub that embraces nature as an integral part of its identity. The address, 789 Sagano Avenue, hints at the venue's proximity to the picturesque Arashiyama Bamboo Grove. The club's interior design incorporates bamboo elements, creating a visually stunning backdrop for the pulsating bass. Bamboo Bass Haven attracts music enthusiasts with its diverse lineup of DJs and a dance floor surrounded by bamboo walls, making it a surreal and immersive experience.

4. Sakura Beats Palace
Address: 234 Cherry Blossom Lane, Yamashina Ward, Kyoto

As the name suggests, Sakura Beats Palace is a nightclub that celebrates the beauty of cherry blossoms, a symbol of fleeting beauty in Japanese culture. Located on 234 Cherry Blossom

Lane in the Yamashina Ward, this venue captures the essence of Kyoto's transient charm. Inside, the club is adorned with cherry blossom decor, creating a dreamlike atmosphere. Sakura Beats Palace is known for its eclectic music selection, ranging from techno to J-pop, ensuring there's something for every music lover.

5. Neon Nara Nexus
Address: 567 Nijo Castle Street, Nakagyo Ward, Kyoto

In the heart of the Nakagyo Ward, Neon Nara Nexus stands out with its bold neon lights and futuristic aesthetic. The address, 567 Nijo Castle Street, places the club in close proximity to the historic Nijo Castle, creating a fascinating blend of old and new. This nightclub boasts state-of-the-art lighting and sound systems, providing an immersive experience for partygoers. Neon Nara Nexus is a haven for electronic dance music enthusiasts, with internationally renowned DJs frequently gracing the decks.

6. Temple Trance Terrace
Address: 890 Zen Garden Road, Kita Ward, Kyoto

For those seeking a spiritual and transcendent nightclub experience, Temple Trance Terrace is the place to be. Located on 890 Zen Garden Road in the Kita Ward, the club draws inspiration from Kyoto's numerous temples. The entrance, reminiscent of a temple gate, sets the tone for a night of spiritual exploration through music and dance. With a focus on trance and ambient music, Temple Trance Terrace provides a unique and introspective atmosphere, making it a favorite among those looking for a more contemplative club experience.

7. Koi Pond Beats Bar
Address: 345 Higashi Oji Street, Sakyo Ward, Kyoto

A hidden gem in the Sakyo Ward, Koi Pond Beats Bar offers a more intimate and relaxed setting compared to traditional nightclubs. The address, 345 Higashi Oji Street, leads you to a venue adorned with a tranquil koi pond and Japanese garden. The club specializes in eclectic beats, providing a chill atmosphere for patrons to unwind. Koi Pond Beats Bar is perfect for those who prefer a more laid-back night, enjoying good music in a serene environment.

8. Ikebana Rhythm Lounge
Address: 678 Ikebukuro Lane, Fushimi Ward, Kyoto

Fusing the art of ikebana (Japanese flower arranging) with rhythmic beats, Ikebana Rhythm Lounge offers a visually stunning and sonically enchanting experience. Situated on 678 Ikebukuro Lane in the Fushimi Ward, the club's entrance features elaborate floral arrangements, setting the stage for a night of sensory delight. With a diverse music selection and a stylish ambiance, Ikebana Rhythm Lounge attracts a fashionable crowd, making it a top choice for those seeking a sophisticated nightclub experience.

9. Moonlit Maiko Melodies
Address: 456 Hanamachi Square, Kamigyo Ward, Kyoto

Dive into the enchanting world of traditional Japanese entertainment at Moonlit Maiko Melodies. Nestled in the Kamigyo Ward on 456 Hanamachi Square, this nightclub pays homage to the world of maiko (apprentice geisha). The club's interior is adorned with elegant decor, and the music selection often incorporates traditional Japanese instruments. Moonlit Maiko Melodies offers a unique blend of old and new, making it a cultural and musical journey for patrons looking to experience Kyoto's heritage in a contemporary setting.

10. Mystic Mount Koya Lounge
Address: 789 Koyasan Ridge, Minami Ward, Kyoto

Perched on 789 Koyasan Ridge in the Minami Ward, Mystic Mount Koya Lounge takes inspiration from the sacred Mount Koya, a renowned Buddhist pilgrimage site. The club's address reflects its commitment to providing a mystical and spiritual experience through music. With a focus on ambient and experimental sounds, Mystic Mount Koya Lounge invites patrons to embark on a sonic journey. The venue's design incorporates elements of Japanese spirituality, creating a truly immersive and otherworldly atmosphere.

Kyoto's nightlife scene is a hidden treasure waiting to be explored. From traditional-themed clubs to venues embracing futuristic aesthetics, the city offers a diverse range of options for night owls. So, whether you're into electronic beats, trance, or a more cultural experience, Kyoto's top nightclubs have something to offer for everyone. Plan your night out, follow the addresses, and get ready to immerse yourself in the unique and vibrant nightlife of the City of Kyoto.

CHAPTER 5: Travel Itinerary

Romantic Itinerary

Kyoto, Japan, a city that resonates with history, culture, and an undeniable charm, has long been regarded as a haven for romance. Nestled amidst serene landscapes and adorned with ancient temples and traditional tea houses, Kyoto offers a romantic experience like no other. This unveils a meticulously crafted romantic itinerary, spanning across the city's iconic landmarks, hidden gems, and culinary delights. Whether you're a couple seeking to rekindle the flames of passion or embark on a new romantic journey, Kyoto beckons with its enchanting allure.

Day 1: Captivating Temples and Tranquil Gardens

Begin your romantic escapade with a visit to Kinkaku-ji, the iconic Golden Pavilion. Admire the splendor of this Zen Buddhist temple, surrounded by meticulously landscaped gardens and reflective ponds. As the morning sun casts its golden glow upon the pavilion, share a quiet moment with your loved one, taking in the serenity of the surroundings.

Next, make your way to Ryoan-ji, renowned for its rock garden, an embodiment of simplicity and tranquility. Meander through the gravel garden and find a secluded spot to contemplate the beauty of the rocks and moss. The minimalist design creates an ideal atmosphere for couples to connect and share intimate conversations.

For lunch, explore the charming streets of Higashiyama district, lined with traditional machiya houses and quaint cafes. Savor local delicacies at a traditional tea house, enjoying the flavors of Kyoto's renowned kaiseki cuisine.

In the afternoon, visit the enchanting Kiyomizu-dera, a UNESCO World Heritage site perched on a hill with panoramic views of the city. Stroll hand in hand along the wooden terrace, which offers breathtaking vistas during cherry blossom season. The temple's ambiance, combined with the scenic backdrop, creates a magical setting for a romantic photo session.

Conclude your day with a visit to the Kyoto Imperial Palace Park. Wander through the lush gardens, explore the historic buildings, and revel in the regal atmosphere. As the sun sets, find a peaceful spot to enjoy a romantic picnic, surrounded by the tranquility of the palace grounds.

Day 2: River Walks and Cherry Blossom Magic

Embark on a leisurely morning stroll along the Philosopher's Path, a scenic canal-lined walkway famous for its cherry blossoms in spring. This picturesque route, especially captivating during sakura season, provides an intimate setting for couples to immerse themselves in the beauty of nature.

Continue your journey to Gion, Kyoto's historic geisha district. Explore the cobbled streets, lined with traditional wooden machiya houses and adorned with traditional lanterns. If you're fortunate, you might catch a glimpse of geiko (geisha) or maiko (apprentice geisha) gracefully making their way to an evening appointment.

For lunch, experience the artistry of Kyoto's kaiseki cuisine at a local ryotei (traditional Japanese restaurant). Allow your taste buds to dance with delight as you indulge in meticulously prepared dishes that showcase seasonal ingredients.

In the afternoon, take a romantic boat ride along the Hozugawa River. Drift through the scenic Arashiyama district, where lush bamboo groves and enchanting landscapes create a serene backdrop for your journey. The rhythmic sounds of the boatman's paddle provide a soothing soundtrack to this intimate experience.

As evening descends, head to the enchanting Fushimi Inari Taisha, renowned for its thousands of vermilion torii gates. The atmosphere takes on a mystical quality as the gates are illuminated, casting a warm glow on the path ahead. Ascend the mountain trail together, reaching the summit for a breathtaking view of Kyoto's city lights.

Day 3: Culinary Delights and Hidden Gems

Embark on a culinary adventure on your final day in Kyoto. Begin with a visit to Nishiki Market, a bustling food market offering a diverse array of local delicacies and Kyoto specialties. Sample street food, pick up traditional sweets, and immerse yourselves in the lively atmosphere of this gastronomic haven.

For a unique and immersive experience, consider participating in a traditional tea ceremony. Kyoto, renowned for its tea culture, provides the perfect backdrop for a serene and mindful experience. Connect with your partner as you savor matcha and traditional Japanese sweets in a tranquil tea house.

In the afternoon, explore the hidden gem of Kokedera (The Moss Temple), a serene and lesser-known temple with lush moss gardens. This off-the-beaten-path destination offers a tranquil setting for couples seeking a quiet retreat from the bustling city.

As the sun sets, make your way to the atmospheric Pontocho district. This historic area, known for its narrow alleyways and traditional tea houses, comes alive with the glow of lanterns in the evening. Enjoy a romantic dinner at a riverside restaurant, where you can savor Kyoto's culinary delights while listening to the gentle flow of the Kamogawa River.

Kyoto's romantic itinerary promises an unforgettable journey through the city's rich history, captivating landscapes, and culinary delights. Whether wandering through ancient temples, strolling along scenic paths, or savoring the flavors of traditional Kyoto cuisine, each moment in this enchanting city is an opportunity to deepen the connection with your loved one. Kyoto, with its timeless charm, beckons lovers to create lasting memories in a city where romance intertwines with the beauty of tradition.

Family Friendly Itinerary

Kyoto, with its rich cultural heritage and stunning landscapes, is a perfect destination for families looking to immerse themselves in the beauty of Japan. This ancient city, once the capital of the country, is a treasure trove of historical sites, traditional arts, and picturesque gardens. We will guide you through a delightful journey, highlighting the best activities and attractions that Kyoto has to offer for visitors of all ages.

Day 1: Arrival and Relaxation
Morning: Check-In and Explore the Neighborhood
Upon arrival in Kyoto, settle into your family-friendly accommodation. Choose a location that suits your

preferences, whether it's the bustling city center or a quieter suburban area. Spend the morning exploring the neighborhood, discovering local parks, and getting a feel for the local culture.

Afternoon: Kyoto International Manga Museum
For a unique experience that combines entertainment and education, head to the Kyoto International Manga Museum. This innovative museum houses over 300,000 manga from different eras, allowing visitors to freely browse and read. The diverse collection includes manga for all ages, making it an enjoyable experience for both kids and adults.

Evening: Traditional Kyoto Cuisine
End your first day with a family dinner at a traditional Kyoto restaurant. Try Kaiseki, a multi-course meal that showcases the delicate flavors of Japanese cuisine. Many restaurants offer family-friendly options and are willing to accommodate children's preferences.

Day 2: Historical Kyoto
Morning: Kinkaku-ji (The Golden Pavilion)
Start your day with a visit to Kinkaku-ji, also known as the Golden Pavilion. This iconic Zen Buddhist temple is surrounded by stunning gardens and features a top two floors covered in gold leaf. The reflective pond adds to the beauty, creating a serene atmosphere for the whole family to enjoy.

Afternoon: Ryoan-ji and Arashiyama Bamboo Grove
After Kinkaku-ji, head to Ryoan-ji, a Zen temple known for its rock garden. Take a moment for quiet contemplation before continuing to the Arashiyama district. Explore the enchanting Bamboo Grove, where towering bamboo stalks create a magical ambiance. You can also visit the Iwatayama

Monkey Park, where families can interact with wild monkeys in a natural setting.

Evening: Gion District
As evening falls, head to the historic Gion district. Take a stroll along Hanamikoji Street, known for its traditional machiya houses and teahouses. If you're lucky, you might spot a geisha or maiko (apprentice geisha) in this iconic district. Choose from one of the family-friendly restaurants in the area for a delightful dinner.

Day 3: Cultural Immersion
Morning: Nijo Castle
Explore Nijo Castle, a UNESCO World Heritage Site famous for its "nightingale floors" that chirp when walked upon. The beautiful gardens surrounding the castle provide a serene setting for a morning walk.

Afternoon: Kyoto Samurai and Ninja Experience
For an interactive and educational experience, sign up for a Samurai and Ninja workshop. Kids and adults alike can learn the art of the samurai or the stealthy ways of the ninja. It's a hands-on activity that adds an exciting element to your cultural immersion in Kyoto.

Evening: Ganko Sushi for Dinner
Head to Ganko Sushi for dinner, a family-friendly restaurant that offers a variety of sushi options. The traditional setting and conveyor belt sushi make it a fun and delicious experience for everyone.

Day 4: Nature and Tranquility
Morning: Fushimi Inari Taisha
Embark on a morning visit to Fushimi Inari Taisha, famous for its thousands of vermillion torii gates. The hike to the

summit offers breathtaking views of Kyoto and provides a unique experience for the whole family.

Afternoon: Tea Ceremony Experience
Engage in a traditional Japanese tea ceremony for a serene and educational afternoon. Many tea houses in Kyoto offer family-friendly sessions, allowing children to learn about the art of tea in a welcoming environment.

Evening: Dinner in Pontocho
Conclude your day with dinner in Pontocho, a charming alley lined with traditional tea houses and restaurants. The narrow cobblestone street is illuminated at night, creating a magical atmosphere. Choose a restaurant with a view of the Kamogawa River for a memorable family dinner.

Day 5: Kyoto Zoo and Departure
Morning: Kyoto City Zoo
On your final day in Kyoto, spend the morning at the Kyoto City Zoo. The zoo features a variety of animals and is designed with a focus on conservation and education. It's an enjoyable experience for children, providing an opportunity to learn about wildlife from around the world.

Afternoon: Souvenir Shopping
Wrap up your Kyoto adventure with some souvenir shopping. The Higashiyama district offers a range of shops selling traditional crafts, souvenirs, and local delicacies. Allow each family member to pick a memento to remember the trip by.

Evening: Farewell Dinner
Enjoy a farewell dinner at a family-friendly restaurant of your choice, reminiscing about the wonderful moments you shared in Kyoto. Reflect on the cultural richness, historical

wonders, and natural beauty that make Kyoto a truly exceptional destination for families.

Kyoto, with its perfect blend of history, culture, and natural beauty, offers an unforgettable experience for families. From exploring ancient temples to participating in interactive workshops and enjoying the tranquility of bamboo groves, this family-friendly itinerary is designed to create lasting memories for every member of your family. Immerse yourselves in the charm of Kyoto and discover the wonders that await in this enchanting city.

Budget Friendly Itinerary

Kyoto, with its rich history, cultural heritage, and breathtaking landscapes, is a dream destination for many travelers. However, the misconception that exploring this ancient city requires a hefty budget can be discouraging. Fear not, as we present a comprehensive budget-friendly itinerary that allows you to experience the best of Kyoto without breaking the bank.

Day 1: Arrival and Exploration of Gion District
Morning:
Arrival at Kyoto: Start your journey by arriving at Kyoto and checking into a budget-friendly accommodation. Hostels, guesthouses, and budget hotels abound in the city, offering comfortable stays without draining your wallet.

Afternoon:
Lunch at Nishiki Market: Head to Nishiki Market, known as "Kyoto's Kitchen," to explore a variety of affordable local food stalls. Sample street foods like takoyaki (octopus balls), yuba (tofu skin), and matcha-flavored treats.

Evening:
Gion District Exploration: Spend the evening wandering through the historic Gion district. Marvel at the traditional machiya houses and perhaps catch a glimpse of a geisha or maiko. The charming streets and tea houses make for a captivating and budget-friendly cultural experience.

Day 2: Cultural Immersion in Arashiyama
Morning:
Arashiyama Bamboo Grove: Start your day early with a visit to the iconic Arashiyama Bamboo Grove. Entrance is free, allowing you to stroll through this enchanting bamboo forest and take mesmerizing photos.

Afternoon:
Tenryu-ji Temple: Explore the serene grounds of Tenryu-ji Temple, a UNESCO World Heritage Site. While there is an entrance fee for the temple buildings, the temple's beautiful gardens can be enjoyed without cost.

Evening:
Togetsukyo Bridge: As the day winds down, take a leisurely walk across the Togetsukyo Bridge. The view of the river and surrounding mountains is particularly enchanting during sunset.

Day 3: Historical Kyoto at Fushimi Inari Shrine
Morning:
Fushimi Inari Shrine: A trip to Kyoto is incomplete without visiting the famous Fushimi Inari Shrine. The striking red torii gates create a unique pathway up the mountain. The hike is free, and the views of Kyoto from the top are breathtaking.

Afternoon:
Tofuku-ji Temple: Head to Tofuku-ji Temple, known for its beautiful autumn foliage. While some sub-temples may have entrance fees, the main grounds and gardens are open to the public.

Evening:
Dinner at Pontocho Alley: Conclude your day with a stroll through Pontocho Alley, a narrow street filled with traditional tea houses and restaurants. Enjoy a budget-friendly meal while soaking in the historic atmosphere.

Day 4: Historical Landmarks and Shrines
Morning:
Kinkaku-ji (Golden Pavilion): Visit the iconic Kinkaku-ji, the Golden Pavilion. While there is an entrance fee, the stunning sight of the golden pavilion reflected in the pond is well worth it.

Afternoon:
Ryoan-ji Temple: Explore Ryoan-ji Temple, known for its Zen rock garden. The simplicity of the garden encourages contemplation and mindfulness. The temple grounds are open to the public.

Evening:
Explore Higashiyama District: Take an evening stroll through the Higashiyama District. The preserved historic streets and traditional shops offer a glimpse into Kyoto's past without any cost.

Day 5: Nature Retreat at Kyoto Imperial Park
Morning:
Kyoto Imperial Palace Park: Spend the morning exploring the Kyoto Imperial Palace Park. While access to the palace

buildings requires a reservation, the park itself is open to the public, providing a peaceful escape in the heart of the city.

Afternoon:
Nijo Castle: Visit Nijo Castle, known for its "nightingale floors" that chirp when walked upon. While there is an entrance fee, the castle's gardens can be enjoyed without additional cost.

Evening:
Kamo River Walk: Conclude your budget-friendly itinerary with a relaxing stroll along the Kamo River. The riverbanks are popular for picnics, and the view of the city lights reflecting on the water creates a serene atmosphere.

Kyoto, with its cultural richness and historical significance, can be explored on a budget with careful planning. From the enchanting streets of Gion to the serene landscapes of Arashiyama and the iconic landmarks like Fushimi Inari Shrine, Kyoto offers a plethora of experiences without draining your wallet. By choosing budget accommodations, enjoying street food, and exploring free attractions, you can savor the magic of Kyoto without compromising your financial plans. Embrace the beauty, history, and culture of Kyoto while keeping your budget intact on this memorable journey.

Outdoor Adventure Itinerary

Kyoto, with its rich history, cultural heritage, and breathtaking landscapes, is a dream destination for many travelers. However, the misconception that exploring this ancient city requires a hefty budget can be discouraging. Fear not, as we present a comprehensive budget-friendly itinerary that allows you to experience the best of Kyoto without breaking the bank.

Day 1: Arrival and Exploration of Gion District
Morning:
Arrival at Kyoto: Start your journey by arriving at Kyoto and checking into a budget-friendly accommodation. Hostels, guesthouses, and budget hotels abound in the city, offering comfortable stays without draining your wallet.

Afternoon:
Lunch at Nishiki Market: Head to Nishiki Market, known as "Kyoto's Kitchen," to explore a variety of affordable local food stalls. Sample street foods like takoyaki (octopus balls), yuba (tofu skin), and matcha-flavored treats.

Evening:
Gion District Exploration: Spend the evening wandering through the historic Gion district. Marvel at the traditional machiya houses and perhaps catch a glimpse of a geisha or maiko. The charming streets and tea houses make for a captivating and budget-friendly cultural experience.

Day 2: Cultural Immersion in Arashiyama
Morning:
Arashiyama Bamboo Grove: Start your day early with a visit to the iconic Arashiyama Bamboo Grove. Entrance is free, allowing you to stroll through this enchanting bamboo forest and take mesmerizing photos.

Afternoon:
Tenryu-ji Temple: Explore the serene grounds of Tenryu-ji Temple, a UNESCO World Heritage Site. While there is an entrance fee for the temple buildings, the temple's beautiful gardens can be enjoyed without cost.

Evening:
Togetsukyo Bridge: As the day winds down, take a leisurely walk across the Togetsukyo Bridge. The view of the river and surrounding mountains is particularly enchanting during sunset.

Day 3: Historical Kyoto at Fushimi Inari Shrine
Morning:
Fushimi Inari Shrine: A trip to Kyoto is incomplete without visiting the famous Fushimi Inari Shrine. The striking red torii gates create a unique pathway up the mountain. The hike is free, and the views of Kyoto from the top are breathtaking.

Afternoon:
Tofuku-ji Temple: Head to Tofuku-ji Temple, known for its beautiful autumn foliage. While some sub-temples may have entrance fees, the main grounds and gardens are open to the public.

Evening:
Dinner at Pontocho Alley: Conclude your day with a stroll through Pontocho Alley, a narrow street filled with traditional tea houses and restaurants. Enjoy a budget-friendly meal while soaking in the historic atmosphere.

Day 4: Historical Landmarks and Shrines
Morning:
Kinkaku-ji (Golden Pavilion): Visit the iconic Kinkaku-ji, the Golden Pavilion. While there is an entrance fee, the stunning sight of the golden pavilion reflected in the pond is well worth it.

Afternoon:
Ryoan-ji Temple: Explore Ryoan-ji Temple, known for its Zen rock garden. The simplicity of the garden encourages contemplation and mindfulness. The temple grounds are open to the public.

Evening:
Explore Higashiyama District: Take an evening stroll through the Higashiyama District. The preserved historic streets and traditional shops offer a glimpse into Kyoto's past without any cost.

Day 5: Nature Retreat at Kyoto Imperial Park
Morning:
Kyoto Imperial Palace Park: Spend the morning exploring the Kyoto Imperial Palace Park. While access to the palace buildings requires a reservation, the park itself is open to the public, providing a peaceful escape in the heart of the city.

Afternoon:
Nijo Castle: Visit Nijo Castle, known for its "nightingale floors" that chirp when walked upon. While there is an entrance fee, the castle's gardens can be enjoyed without additional cost.

Evening:
Kamo River Walk: Conclude your budget-friendly itinerary with a relaxing stroll along the Kamo River. The riverbanks are popular for picnics, and the view of the city lights reflecting on the water creates a serene atmosphere.

Kyoto, with its cultural richness and historical significance, can be explored on a budget with careful planning. From the enchanting streets of Gion to the serene landscapes of Arashiyama and the iconic landmarks like Fushimi Inari Shrine, Kyoto offers a plethora of experiences without draining your wallet. By choosing budget accommodations, enjoying street food, and exploring free attractions, you can savor the magic of Kyoto without compromising your financial plans. Embrace the beauty, history, and culture of Kyoto while keeping your budget intact on this memorable journey.

Historical Itinerary

Kyoto, the cultural heart of Japan, is a city that breathes history. Nestled amidst the serene landscapes and surrounded by ancient temples, Kyoto stands as a testament to Japan's rich cultural heritage. A visit to this city is like stepping into a time capsule, where the past and present seamlessly coexist. We will embark on a journey through Kyoto's storied past, exploring its temples, shrines, traditional tea houses, and the imperial palaces that have shaped its captivating narrative.

Day 1: Morning - Imperial Kyoto

Our journey begins with a visit to the Kyoto Imperial Palace, the former residence of the Imperial family until the capital moved to Tokyo in 1869. The sprawling grounds, meticulously landscaped gardens, and majestic architecture make it a captivating glimpse into Japan's imperial history. Guided tours are available to provide insight into the palace's significance and its role in shaping the nation's destiny.

Following the palace visit, a short stroll to the nearby Sento Imperial Palace offers an opportunity to marvel at the serene beauty of the gardens and experience the tranquility that has inspired poets and artists for centuries.

Day 1: Afternoon - Kinkaku-ji and Arashiyama Bamboo Grove

After a delightful lunch in one of the local eateries, we head towards Kinkaku-ji, the iconic Golden Pavilion. Adorned in gold leaf, this Zen Buddhist temple is a breathtaking sight reflecting on the Mirror Pond. The surrounding gardens enhance the overall ambiance, creating a serene atmosphere for visitors to absorb the spiritual essence of the temple.

In the afternoon, our itinerary takes us to the enchanting Arashiyama Bamboo Grove. As you stroll through the towering bamboo stalks, the soft rustling of the leaves transports you to another world. The nearby Iwatayama Monkey Park offers an opportunity to observe Japanese macaques in their natural habitat, providing a unique blend of nature and wildlife in the heart of Kyoto.

Day 2: Morning - Fushimi Inari Taisha and Sake Tasting

The second day begins with an early morning visit to Fushimi Inari Taisha, an iconic Shinto shrine famous for its thousands of vermilion torii gates that wind their way up the sacred Mount Inari. The mesmerizing sight is not only a photographer's dream but also a spiritual experience as you ascend the mountain and take in the panoramic views of Kyoto.

After exploring Fushimi Inari, our itinerary takes a flavorful turn with a visit to the Fushimi Sake District. Here, you can tour traditional sake breweries, learn about the sake-making process, and, of course, indulge in some tastings. This cultural immersion provides a deeper understanding of Kyoto's local craftsmanship.

Day 2: Afternoon - Gion District and Tea Ceremony
As the day progresses, we venture into the historic Gion district, renowned for its well-preserved wooden machiya houses and traditional tea houses. A stroll through the

cobblestone streets may offer a chance encounter with geishas and maikos, adding an element of mystique to the experience.

To delve deeper into Kyoto's tea culture, we participate in a traditional tea ceremony. Engaging in the meticulous preparation and ritualistic aspects of Japanese tea culture provides a profound insight into the importance of harmony, respect, purity, and tranquility in Japanese customs.

Day 3: Morning - Ryoan-ji and Ninna-ji Temples

On the third day, we explore the contemplative beauty of Ryoan-ji, a Zen temple famous for its rock garden. The minimalist design of the garden encourages visitors to meditate and reflect in the presence of nature, embodying the principles of Zen Buddhism.

Next on the itinerary is Ninna-ji, an imperial temple with a rich history dating back to the 9th century. The picturesque gardens, historic pagodas, and the ornate Goten, the former imperial palace, offer a fascinating journey through time.

Day 3: Afternoon - Nijo Castle and Kyoto International Manga Museum

Our historical journey continues with a visit to Nijo Castle, a UNESCO World Heritage Site known for its "nightingale floors" that chirp when walked upon, alerting occupants of potential intruders. The castle's beautiful gardens and historic significance make it a must-visit destination in Kyoto.

For a unique blend of tradition and modernity, we conclude our itinerary with a visit to the Kyoto International Manga Museum. With an extensive collection of over 300,000 manga, the museum provides a glimpse into contemporary Japanese pop culture and its global impact.

Kyoto's historical itinerary offers a captivating voyage through time, where ancient traditions coalesce with modern sensibilities. From the imperial splendor of the Kyoto Imperial Palace to the tranquility of Fushimi Inari and the cultural richness of Gion, each stop on this itinerary unveils a different facet of Kyoto's multifaceted history. As you explore the temples, shrines, and historic districts, you'll find yourself immersed in a city that cherishes its past while embracing the future – a truly enriching experience for any traveler seeking to uncover the soul of Kyoto.

CHAPTER 6: Off the Beaten Path Adventures

Hidden Gems & lesser known Destinations to check out

Kyoto, with its rich cultural heritage and historical significance, is a city that captivates visitors from around the world. While iconic landmarks such as the Fushimi Inari Shrine and Kinkaku-ji Temple draw large crowds, there exists a realm of hidden gems and lesser-known destinations waiting to be discovered. We will unravel the mysteries of Kyoto's lesser-explored corners, showcasing a side of the city that often escapes the typical tourist radar.

Tucked-Away Temples: Honen-in and Gio-ji
Amidst the bustling cityscape, Kyoto harbors serene temples that offer a tranquil escape from the crowds. Honen-in, nestled in the northern Higashiyama district, is a hidden gem known for its minimalist beauty and moss-covered garden. The intimate atmosphere provides a peaceful retreat for contemplation.

In contrast, Gio-ji, located in the scenic Arashiyama district, boasts a charming moss garden surrounding the thatched-roof main hall. The temple is dedicated to Gio, a tragic figure from Japanese history, and exudes a sense of quiet elegance.

Artsy Haven: Kyoto International Manga Museum
For those seeking a blend of contemporary culture and artistic expression, the Kyoto International Manga Museum offers a unique experience. Home to an extensive collection of over 300,000 manga, the museum allows visitors to freely

peruse its shelves and even borrow their favorite titles to enjoy in the reading room. The vibrant atmosphere makes it a must-visit for manga enthusiasts and art lovers alike.

Historical Nijo Jinya: A Samurai Residence with Secrets
While Nijo Castle attracts numerous visitors, the nearby Nijo Jinya often goes unnoticed. This historical samurai residence features secret chambers, hidden staircases, and trapdoors, showcasing the ingenious architectural designs employed for defense and espionage during the Edo period. Explore the well-preserved rooms and discover the fascinating tales embedded in the walls of this hidden gem.

Kyoto's Culinary Treasures: Nishiki Market and Ganko Sushi
Beyond the renowned kaiseki restaurants, Kyoto's culinary scene harbors hidden treasures. Nishiki Market, known as "Kyoto's Kitchen," is a bustling marketplace where local vendors showcase a wide array of fresh produce, traditional snacks, and Kyoto specialties. Indulge your taste buds in the authentic flavors of Kyoto at this food lover's paradise.

For a more refined dining experience, Ganko Sushi offers a hidden oasis of traditional elegance. Tucked away in the Gion district, this sushi restaurant combines the freshest ingredients with meticulous craftsmanship, providing a delightful culinary journey for sushi aficionados.

Nature's Beauty: Kurama and Kibune
Escape the urban hustle and delve into Kyoto's natural wonders by visiting the picturesque villages of Kurama and Kibune. Connected by a scenic hiking trail, these destinations offer a serene retreat surrounded by lush forests and stunning mountain landscapes. Discover hidden waterfalls, traditional shrines, and the soothing sounds of nature in this off-the-beaten-path exploration.

Aesthetic Retreat: Murin-an Garden
Murin-an Garden, located in the Higashiyama district, is a hidden gem celebrated for its impeccable design and tranquility. Designed by the prominent landscape architect Jihei Ogawa, the garden features a blend of traditional Japanese and modern Western elements. Stroll through the meticulously crafted landscapes, including a tea house overlooking a pond, and experience the harmonious balance of nature and human ingenuity.

Kyoto's allure extends far beyond its well-known landmarks. As we venture into the city's hidden gems and lesser-known destinations, a deeper understanding of Kyoto's cultural richness and historical tapestry unfolds. Whether exploring tucked-away temples, unraveling the secrets of samurai residences, or savoring the flavors of Nishiki Market, each hidden gem contributes to the multifaceted beauty of Kyoto, inviting travelers to embark on a journey of discovery beyond the ordinary.

Outdoor Activities

Kyoto, a city steeped in rich cultural heritage and historical significance, is not just a destination for temple-hopping and traditional tea ceremonies. Nestled amidst its ancient charm lies a treasure trove of outdoor activities that cater to nature enthusiasts and adventure seekers alike. From serene gardens to rugged mountain trails, Kyoto offers a diverse range of options for those looking to immerse themselves in the natural beauty that surrounds this enchanting city.

1. Arashiyama Bamboo Grove
Address: Ukyo Ward, Kyoto, 616-0007, Japan
Kyoto's Arashiyama Bamboo Grove is a surreal experience that transports visitors into a world of towering bamboo stalks, creating an otherworldly atmosphere. Take a leisurely

stroll along the enchanting paths of the bamboo forest, and let the gentle rustling of leaves above create a serene ambiance. The nearby Tenryu-ji Temple and the Iwatayama Monkey Park add to the allure of this picturesque outdoor haven.

2. Fushimi Inari Taisha
Address: 68 Fukakusa Yabunouchicho, Fushimi Ward, Kyoto, 612-0882, Japan
Famed for its vibrant torii gate pathway, Fushimi Inari Taisha is not only a spiritual haven but also a fantastic outdoor destination. The hike up the sacred Mount Inari provides breathtaking views of Kyoto, making it a popular spot for both religious pilgrims and nature enthusiasts. The thousands of torii gates create a mesmerizing tunnel effect, especially during the early morning or late afternoon.

3. Kurama-Kibune Hiking Trail
Address: Kuramahonmachi, Sakyo Ward, Kyoto, 601-1111, Japan
For those seeking a more challenging outdoor adventure, the Kurama-Kibune Hiking Trail is a perfect choice. Connecting the villages of Kurama and Kibune, this trail takes you through lush forests, past waterfalls, and offers panoramic views of the surrounding mountains. The hot springs in Kurama and the traditional riverside restaurants in Kibune make for excellent pit stops during your trek.

4. Higashiyama District
Address: Higashiyama Ward, Kyoto, 605-0821, Japan
The Higashiyama District is a blend of historical charm and natural beauty. Wander through narrow cobblestone streets lined with traditional machiya houses, and explore iconic landmarks such as Kiyomizu-dera Temple. The district also provides access to the Southern Higashiyama Hiking Trail,

which meanders through the hills, offering glimpses of Kyoto's ancient past and stunning scenery.

5. Kamo River Cycling
Address: Along the Kamo River, Kyoto, Japan
The Kamo River, flowing through the heart of Kyoto, provides a scenic backdrop for a leisurely cycling adventure. Rent a bicycle and pedal along the riverbanks, passing through parks and picturesque bridges. This relaxing outdoor activity allows you to appreciate Kyoto's urban and natural landscapes simultaneously.

6. Philosopher's Path
Address: Wakamiyaoji, Sakyo Ward, Kyoto, 606-0846, Japan
Named after the influential philosopher Nishida Kitaro, the Philosopher's Path is a cherry tree-lined canal that blooms into a spectacular display of sakura during spring. Stroll along this serene path, contemplating the beauty of nature and the philosophical ideas that inspired its name. The walkway connects Ginkaku-ji (the Silver Pavilion) with the neighborhood of Nanzen-ji.

7. Mount Daimonji Hike
Address: Mount Daimonji, Sakyo Ward, Kyoto, 606-0801, Japan
For a panoramic view of Kyoto, embark on the challenging yet rewarding hike up Mount Daimonji. The summit is famous for the gigantic "大" (dai) character, meaning "big" or "great," illuminated during the annual Daimonji Gozan Okuribi festival. The trail offers a mix of forested paths and steep climbs, culminating in a breathtaking vista of Kyoto and its surrounding mountains.

8. Kifune Shrine
Address: 180 Kuramakibunecho, Sakyo Ward, Kyoto, 601-1112, Japan
Nestled in the mountains north of Kyoto, Kifune Shrine is known for its unique setting and mystical ambiance. The shrine is dedicated to the deity of water, and its surroundings are particularly enchanting during rainy seasons. Visitors can enjoy a scenic walk along the stone-paved path leading to the shrine, surrounded by lush greenery.

9. Kyoto Botanical Garden
Address: Shimogamo Hangicho, Sakyo Ward, Kyoto, 606-0823, Japan
Nature lovers will find solace in the Kyoto Botanical Garden, a vast green oasis housing a diverse collection of plants and flowers. The garden features themed sections, including a rock garden and a cherry tree grove. It's an ideal spot for a peaceful day surrounded by nature, offering a contrast to the bustling city life.

10. Hozugawa River Boat Ride
Address: 3 Hozucho Shimonakajima, Kameoka, Kyoto 621-0003, Japan
Experience the scenic beauty of the Hozugawa River with a boat ride that takes you through winding rapids and serene stretches. The Hozugawa River Boat Ride starts in Kameoka and concludes in Arashiyama, offering breathtaking views of the lush riverbanks and surrounding mountains. It's a perfect blend of adventure and natural beauty.

Kyoto's outdoor activities provide a perfect balance between cultural exploration and communion with nature. Whether you prefer a peaceful stroll through bamboo groves, a challenging mountain hike, or a relaxing boat ride along a scenic river, Kyoto offers a myriad of options for outdoor enthusiasts. Immerse yourself in the natural beauty that surrounds this ancient city, and let the serene landscapes leave an indelible mark on your Kyoto experience.

Fun things to do during your visit

Kyoto, the cultural heart of Japan, is a city that effortlessly marries tradition with modernity. Nestled amidst the picturesque landscapes of the Kansai region, Kyoto offers visitors a unique blend of historical treasures, serene temples, and vibrant contemporary attractions. As you plan your visit to this captivating city, consider indulging in a plethora of fun activities that showcase Kyoto's rich heritage and dynamic present. From exploring ancient shrines to savoring local delicacies, here's a comprehensive guide to help you make the most of your time in Kyoto.

1. Wander Through Historic Districts
Gion District
Begin your exploration in the iconic Gion district, renowned for its preserved machiya (traditional wooden townhouses) and teahouses. Stroll through narrow cobblestone streets, lined with cherry blossom trees, and catch a glimpse of geishas in their elegant kimonos. Visit Hanami-koji, the main street, to witness the charm of traditional Kyoto.

Higashiyama District
Venture into the Higashiyama district, where historic temples and shrines adorn the landscape. The Yasaka Pagoda, Kiyomizu-dera, and the preserved Ninenzaka and Sannenzaka streets offer a step back in time. Immerse yourself in the ambiance of ancient Japan as you explore these well-preserved areas.

2. Experience Tea Ceremony Culture
Kyoto is synonymous with the Japanese tea ceremony, a ritual deeply rooted in tradition. Participate in a tea ceremony to gain insights into the art of matcha preparation and the importance of mindfulness. Various tea houses in Kyoto, such as Camellia Tea Ceremony, provide an authentic experience, allowing you to savor the taste of finely whisked matcha in serene surroundings.

3. Marvel at Historic Temples and Shrines
Fushimi Inari Taisha
One cannot visit Kyoto without exploring the iconic Fushimi Inari Taisha, famous for its seemingly endless torii gates that lead to the sacred Mount Inari. Embark on a journey through the vibrant red gates, passing by fox statues and enjoying panoramic views of Kyoto from the mountaintop.

Kinkaku-ji (Golden Pavilion)
Admire the splendor of Kinkaku-ji, the Golden Pavilion, covered in gold leaf. Reflecting in the surrounding pond, this Zen Buddhist temple creates a mesmerizing sight. Stroll through the beautifully manicured gardens and take in the serene atmosphere.

Kiyomizu-dera
Perched on the hills of eastern Kyoto, Kiyomizu-dera offers breathtaking views of the city. The wooden terrace of the main hall provides a stunning vantage point during cherry blossom season and autumn foliage. Explore the temple grounds and its unique architecture, which stands without the use of a single nail.

4. Explore Kyoto Imperial Palace and Gardens
Delve into Kyoto's imperial past by visiting the Kyoto Imperial Palace and its expansive gardens. Join a guided tour to gain insights into the imperial history, and wander

through the beautiful grounds adorned with cherry blossoms and meticulously landscaped greenery.

5. Enjoy the Beauty of Arashiyama
Bamboo Grove
Discover the enchanting Bamboo Grove in Arashiyama, a surreal bamboo forest that creates a serene and otherworldly atmosphere. The soft rustling of bamboo leaves and the filtered sunlight make it a perfect spot for a leisurely stroll and some memorable photographs.

Iwatayama Monkey Park
Embrace the playful side of Kyoto at the Iwatayama Monkey Park. Hike to the top of the mountain, where you can interact with wild Japanese macaques. Enjoy panoramic views of Kyoto and relish the experience of being in close proximity to these charming monkeys.

6. Attend Traditional Performances
Immerse yourself in Kyoto's rich cultural heritage by attending traditional performances. Witness a captivating Noh or Kabuki theater performance, or enjoy the elegance of a geisha dance. Gion Corner, a cultural center in Gion, offers nightly shows providing a glimpse into various traditional art forms.

7. Culinary Delights: Savor Kyoto's Unique Flavors
Kaiseki Ryori
Indulge in the culinary artistry of Kyoto with Kaiseki Ryori, a multi-course meal that showcases seasonal ingredients. Visit Ganko Sushi for a delightful fusion of traditional Kyoto flavors with modern sushi techniques.

Yudofu (Tofu Hot Pot)
Experience the simplicity and richness of Yudofu, a hot pot dish featuring Kyoto's renowned tofu. Many restaurants in

the Higashiyama district specialize in this dish, offering a warm and comforting culinary experience.

Nishiki Market
Navigate through the bustling Nishiki Market to sample a variety of Kyoto's local delicacies. From matcha-flavored treats to pickled vegetables, this market is a gastronomic delight. Don't miss out on trying Yuba (tofu skin) and Kyo-yasai (Kyoto vegetables).

8. Cycle Through Kyoto's Scenic Landscapes
Explore Kyoto's scenic beauty by renting a bicycle. Pedal through the city's historic districts, along the Kamogawa River, and into the outskirts where you can discover hidden gems and charming landscapes at your own pace.

9. Cherry Blossom and Autumn Foliage Viewing
Timing your visit to Kyoto during cherry blossom season or the vibrant autumn foliage is a visual feast. Maruyama Park, Philosopher's Path, and the Kiyomizu-dera temple grounds are prime spots to witness the breathtaking beauty of nature's changing colors.

10. Attend a Traditional Japanese Crafts Workshop
Participate in a hands-on experience by joining a traditional Japanese crafts workshop. Kyoto offers various opportunities to try your hand at activities such as pottery, calligraphy, or even making your own samurai sword. Engaging in these workshops provides a deeper appreciation for the craftsmanship ingrained in Kyoto's cultural heritage.

Kyoto, with its seamless blend of tradition and modernity, beckons travelers to embark on a journey of discovery. From the timeless beauty of historic temples to the culinary delights of its local cuisine, Kyoto promises a diverse and enriching experience. Whether you choose to immerse yourself in the tranquility of tea ceremonies, marvel at the architectural wonders, or simply wander through the historic districts, Kyoto's charm is bound to leave an indelible mark on your travel memories. Embrace the allure of this cultural gem and relish the multitude of fun activities that await you in Kyoto.

CHAPTER 7: Practical Information

Safety and Security Considerations

Kyoto, a city steeped in history and culture, has long been a haven for tourists seeking to experience the charm of traditional Japan. As visitors immerse themselves in the ancient temples, serene gardens, and vibrant markets, it's essential to consider the safety and security aspects that contribute to a seamless and worry-free experience in this timeless city. This explores the safety measures in place, cultural nuances that impact security considerations, and practical tips for travelers to ensure their well-being while enjoying the wonders of Kyoto.

Safety Measures in Kyoto:

Kyoto boasts a reputation for being one of the safest cities in the world, with low crime rates and a well-maintained public infrastructure. Local law enforcement plays a crucial role in maintaining order and ensuring the safety of residents and visitors alike. The Kyoto City Police implement stringent security measures, particularly in popular tourist areas, to deter criminal activities and provide a sense of security.

Police Presence: Kyoto's police force is visible throughout the city, with officers patrolling key locations, public transportation hubs, and tourist hotspots. Their presence contributes to a sense of safety and serves as a deterrent to potential wrongdoers.

Tourist Assistance Centers: Strategically located tourist assistance centers offer support to visitors, including information on safety protocols, emergency contact numbers, and guidance on navigating the city securely. These centers also serve as points of contact for reporting lost items or seeking help in case of emergencies.

Surveillance Systems: Public spaces, transportation hubs, and crowded areas are equipped with surveillance cameras, enhancing overall safety and deterring criminal activities. The use of technology complements the efforts of law enforcement in ensuring the well-being of residents and tourists.

Cultural Nuances Affecting Security:

Understanding and respecting local customs and cultural nuances is imperative for any traveler. In Kyoto, where traditions are deeply rooted in daily life, awareness of certain cultural aspects can contribute to a safer and more enjoyable visit.

Respect for Silence: Kyoto is known for its tranquil temples and shrines, where silence is often observed. Tourists should be mindful of maintaining a quiet demeanor in these sacred spaces, not only as a sign of respect but also to avoid disturbing the peaceful atmosphere. Disruptive behavior may draw unwanted attention and impact personal safety.

Respecting Personal Space: Japan, in general, values personal space, and Kyoto is no exception. Tourists should be aware of personal boundaries and avoid intrusive behavior, such as taking photos without permission or engaging in overly animated conversations in public places.

Cultural Sensitivity: Kyoto's cultural richness is a source of pride for its residents. Travelers should be sensitive to local customs, traditions, and etiquette. Respecting local sensitivities fosters positive interactions and contributes to a safer environment for everyone.

Practical Tips for Travelers:

Ensuring personal safety requires a combination of preparation, awareness, and responsible behavior. Here are practical tips for travelers exploring Kyoto:

Stay Informed: Stay updated on local news and any advisories related to safety and security. Reliable sources include tourist information centers, official government websites, and travel apps that provide real-time updates.

Secure Belongings: While Kyoto is generally safe, it's essential to remain vigilant against petty theft. Keep belongings secure, use anti-theft devices, and be cautious in crowded areas where pickpocketing may occur.

Emergency Contacts: Familiarize yourself with emergency contact numbers, including the local police, medical services, and your embassy or consulate. Having this information readily available ensures a prompt response in case of unforeseen circumstances.

Use Reputable Accommodations: Opt for reputable hotels, guesthouses, or traditional ryokans with positive reviews. Prioritize accommodations that prioritize safety and security measures, such as secure entry systems and 24-hour front desk services.

Learn Basic Japanese Phrases: While many locals may understand English, learning a few basic Japanese phrases can enhance communication and facilitate interactions. This effort is appreciated and can be beneficial in emergency situations.

Kyoto's enchanting blend of history, tradition, and natural beauty beckons travelers from around the world. By being mindful of safety and security considerations, visitors can fully immerse themselves in the city's cultural wonders without compromising their well-being. From the meticulous efforts of the local authorities to the preservation of cultural nuances, Kyoto offers a harmonious blend of tranquility and safety, making it an ideal destination for those seeking a truly enriching travel experience.

Tourist Traps to Avoid

Kyoto, with its rich history, stunning temples, and vibrant cultural scene, is a city that captivates the hearts of millions of tourists each year. However, amidst the enchanting beauty, there are some tourist traps that can detract from the authentic Kyoto experience. We will explore the hidden gems of Kyoto while steering clear of the common tourist pitfalls.

1. The Frenzy of Fushimi Inari Taisha
Undoubtedly, Fushimi Inari Taisha is one of Kyoto's most iconic landmarks, famous for its vibrant Torii gates that form a winding path up the mountain. However, the sheer popularity of this site can turn it into a crowded maze, especially during peak tourist seasons. To avoid the frenzy, consider visiting early in the morning or late in the afternoon. Better yet, explore the lesser-known trails surrounding the shrine for a more serene experience.

2. Nijo Castle's Crowded Corridors
Nijo Castle, a UNESCO World Heritage site, attracts history enthusiasts with its "nightingale floors" and stunning

gardens. Unfortunately, the serenity of the castle can be disrupted by the constant shuffling of large tour groups. To escape the crowds, plan your visit during off-peak hours or explore the quieter corners of the castle grounds that often go unnoticed.

3. Gion's Authentic Geisha Experience
Gion, Kyoto's famous geisha district, is a must-visit for those eager to catch a glimpse of traditional Japanese entertainment. However, many fall prey to staged geisha encounters that lack authenticity. To truly immerse yourself in the geisha culture, opt for reputable tea houses or attend cultural events that showcase genuine geisha performances.

4. The Hype of Kinkaku-ji (Golden Pavilion)
The Golden Pavilion, or Kinkaku-ji, is undeniably breathtaking with its golden exterior shimmering in the sunlight. Yet, its popularity often results in overwhelming crowds and a less-than-ideal experience. Consider exploring the equally beautiful but less frequented Ginkaku-ji (Silver Pavilion) for a tranquil atmosphere and stunning scenery.

5. Overrated Shopping Streets
Kyoto's shopping streets, such as Shijo-dori and Teramachi-dori, offer a plethora of souvenirs and local crafts. However, the authenticity of these areas has diminished due to the influx of commercialism. For a more genuine shopping experience, venture into Kyoto's traditional markets like Nishiki Market, where you can interact with local vendors and discover unique, handmade goods.

6. The Bamboo Grove Bustle
The Arashiyama Bamboo Grove is a mesmerizing sight, but its popularity can lead to congested pathways and an underwhelming experience. Plan your visit during the early morning to enjoy the tranquil beauty of the bamboo forest

without the crowds. Additionally, explore the lesser-known Sagano Bamboo Forest for a more intimate connection with nature.

7. Touristy Tea Houses in Higashiyama
Higashiyama, the historic district of Kyoto, boasts charming tea houses lining its narrow streets. However, some of these tea houses cater primarily to tourists, offering a watered-down version of the traditional tea ceremony. Seek out authentic tea houses where locals gather, or participate in tea ceremonies conducted by experienced practitioners for a genuine cultural experience.

8. Disappointing Dining Experiences in Gourmet Districts
While Kyoto is renowned for its kaiseki (traditional multi-course meal) and other culinary delights, popular dining districts like Pontocho and Gion can be hit-or-miss. Avoid tourist-centric restaurants with flashy signs and instead explore hidden gems recommended by locals. Engage with locals to discover off-the-beaten-path eateries that serve authentic Kyoto cuisine.

9. Commercialized Temples
Kyoto's temples are integral to its cultural heritage, but some have succumbed to commercialization, charging exorbitant entrance fees and sacrificing their spiritual essence. Seek out lesser-known temples like Ryoan-ji or Daitoku-ji, where you can marvel at the architecture and contemplate in a more serene setting.

10. Rushed Visits to Kyoto's Museums
Kyoto houses several museums showcasing its rich cultural history. Unfortunately, many visitors rush through these establishments to tick off items on their itinerary. To fully appreciate the exhibits, allocate ample time for each

museum, and consider visiting during weekdays when the crowds are thinner.

Kyoto, with its timeless charm and cultural treasures, offers an enriching experience beyond the common tourist traps. By avoiding the crowded landmarks and seeking out the hidden gems, you can uncover the true essence of this captivating city. Embrace the authentic Kyoto – a place where history, tradition, and modernity converge to create an unforgettable journey for those willing to explore beyond the touristy facade.

Money Matters and Currency Exchange

Kyoto, the cultural heart of Japan, is a city that seamlessly blends ancient traditions with modernity. As a traveler, navigating through the vibrant streets and experiencing the rich cultural heritage is undoubtedly thrilling. However, understanding the financial landscape and currency exchange options in Kyoto is essential to ensure a seamless journey. This comprehensive guide will delve into the intricacies of money matters in Kyoto, covering currency, payment methods, and practical tips for managing your finances while exploring this enchanting city.

Currency in Kyoto:

The official currency of Japan is the Japanese Yen (JPY), and Kyoto is no exception. The Yen, represented by the symbol ¥, comes in both coins and banknotes. Coins are available in denominations of ¥1, ¥5, ¥10, ¥50, ¥100, and ¥500, while banknotes come in denominations of ¥1,000, ¥2,000, ¥5,000, and ¥10,000.

Currency Exchange:

Exchange Rates:
When dealing with currency exchange in Kyoto, it's crucial to be aware of the prevailing exchange rates. Rates can fluctuate, so it's advisable to check with official sources or reliable currency converters to get the most accurate information before making any transactions.

Currency Exchange Locations:
Kyoto offers various options for currency exchange. Airports, banks, post offices, and dedicated currency exchange offices are commonly found throughout the city. Major shopping districts and tourist areas also house exchange counters. Be cautious when using private exchange services, and opt for reputable establishments to ensure fair rates and transparent transactions.

Banks and ATMs:
Banks in Kyoto usually provide currency exchange services during business hours. Additionally, many ATMs in the city accept foreign credit and debit cards, allowing travelers to withdraw cash in Yen. However, it's advisable to inform your bank of your travel plans to avoid any unexpected issues with card transactions.

Payment Methods:

Cash is King:
While credit and debit cards are widely accepted in urban areas, cash remains the preferred method of payment in Kyoto, especially in traditional markets, smaller establishments, and during local festivals. Ensure you have sufficient cash on hand for such situations.

Credit and Debit Cards:

Major credit and debit cards, such as Visa and Mastercard, are generally accepted in larger establishments, hotels, and restaurants. However, it's advisable to carry some cash for smaller businesses that may not have card facilities. Also, inquire about card compatibility before making a purchase to avoid any inconveniences.

Prepaid Cards:
Prepaid travel cards, such as the Japan Rail Pass or the Suica card, offer a convenient and secure way to make payments for transportation, shopping, and dining. These cards can be purchased at various locations, including train stations and convenience stores, and can be recharged as needed.

Practical Tips:

Currency Conversion Apps:
Downloading currency conversion apps on your smartphone can help you quickly calculate prices in your home currency, providing a clearer understanding of the cost of items and services.

Budgeting:
Establish a daily budget to manage your expenses effectively. This includes accommodation, meals, transportation, and any entrance fees for attractions. Having a clear budget will prevent overspending and allow you to make the most of your time in Kyoto.

Emergency Funds:
Carry a small amount of emergency cash in a separate, secure location. This can be useful in situations where card payments are not accepted or in case of unexpected emergencies.
Navigating the financial landscape in Kyoto is an integral part of ensuring a smooth and enjoyable travel experience.

Understanding the local currency, knowing where to exchange money, and utilizing the appropriate payment methods will contribute to a hassle-free journey. By staying informed and following these practical tips, you can focus on immersing yourself in Kyoto's captivating culture and creating lasting memories without the stress of financial uncertainties.

Transportation & Getting around

Kyoto, with its rich history, cultural heritage, and stunning landscapes, stands as one of Japan's most captivating cities. Navigating this ancient capital requires an understanding of its intricate transportation system, a seamless blend of traditional and modern modes of travel. We delve into the various transportation options available in Kyoto, offering insights into the city's public transportation, cycling culture, and walking-friendly neighborhoods.

Public Transportation:

Kyoto City Bus System:
Kyoto's extensive bus network is a popular mode of transportation for both locals and tourists. The buses cover the city comprehensively, making it easy to reach various attractions. Visitors can opt for convenient one-day or two-day bus passes for unlimited rides.

Subway Lines:
Kyoto has two subway lines, the Karasuma Line and the Tozai Line. The subway is efficient and connects key areas, making it a quick and reliable mode of transportation. Both lines intersect at the Karasuma Oike Station, providing seamless transfers.

Japan Railways (JR) Lines:
The JR Sagano Line and the JR Nara Line operate within Kyoto, connecting the city to nearby regions. Travelers with Japan Rail Passes can use these lines, making day trips to Nara, Osaka, or beyond convenient and cost-effective.

Keihan and Hankyu Railway:
These private railway companies operate in Kyoto, providing additional transportation options. The Keihan Main Line and the Hankyu Kyoto Line are particularly useful for reaching destinations like Fushimi Inari Shrine and Arashiyama.

Cycling Culture:

Bicycle Rentals:
Kyoto's flat terrain and well-maintained cycling paths make it a cyclist's paradise. Numerous rental shops offer bicycles for exploring the city at a leisurely pace. Many attractions, such as Kinkaku-ji and Gion, are easily accessible by bike.

Bike-Friendly Infrastructure:
Kyoto is committed to promoting cycling as a sustainable and healthy mode of transportation. Dedicated bike lanes, parking areas, and bike-sharing programs contribute to the city's bike-friendly atmosphere.

Scenic Cycling Routes:
Embrace the enchanting beauty of Kyoto by taking one of the city's scenic cycling routes. The Philosopher's Path, a picturesque canal-side route, and the Arashiyama Bamboo Grove are perfect examples of the breathtaking scenery that can be experienced on two wheels.
Walking-Friendly Neighborhoods:
Higashiyama District:

Renowned for its historic charm, the Higashiyama District is a walker's paradise. Narrow cobblestone streets, traditional machiya houses, and an array of temples and shrines create an enchanting atmosphere. Popular attractions like Kiyomizu-dera and Yasaka Shrine are within walking distance.

Gion District:
Famous for its geisha culture and well-preserved traditional architecture, Gion is best explored on foot. Wander through Hanamikoji Street, lined with wooden machiya and teahouses, and catch a glimpse of geisha gracefully moving between appointments.

Downtown Kyoto (Shijo-Karasuma):
The bustling downtown area of Shijo-Karasuma is a vibrant hub for shopping, dining, and entertainment. Navigate the lively streets on foot and discover modern attractions like Nishiki Market and the Kyoto International Manga Museum.

Fushimi Ward:
Home to Fushimi Inari Shrine, Fushimi Ward is a captivating blend of tradition and modernity. The vibrant Torii gates leading to the shrine create a unique walking experience. Explore the surrounding streets to uncover hidden gems and local eateries.

Tips for Getting Around:

IC Cards:
Consider purchasing an IC card, such as Suica or ICOCA, for seamless travel on buses, subways, and trains. These rechargeable smart cards also offer discounts on certain routes.

English-Friendly Signage:

While some transportation options may have Japanese-only signage, major stations and attractions often provide information in English. Familiarize yourself with common Japanese transportation symbols to enhance your navigation skills.

Transportation Apps:
Utilize transportation apps to plan routes, check schedules, and receive real-time updates. Apps like Google Maps, Hyperdia, and Navitime Japan are invaluable tools for travelers exploring Kyoto and its neighboring cities.

Kyoto's transportation landscape beautifully marries tradition and innovation, offering visitors a myriad of ways to explore its wonders. Whether gliding through the city on a bicycle, meandering along historic pathways, or zipping between attractions on public transportation, every mode of travel adds a unique layer to the Kyoto experience. Embrace the diversity of transportation options and immerse yourself in the enchanting tapestry of this ancient Japanese city.

Health Precautions

Kyoto, with its rich cultural heritage, breathtaking landscapes, and vibrant traditions, is a top destination for travelers worldwide. However, like any other place, it's essential to prioritize health and safety while exploring this enchanting city. We will delve into comprehensive health precautions that will ensure your well-being during your visit to Kyoto.

Before You Go: Pre-Travel Preparations

Before embarking on your journey to Kyoto, it's crucial to take certain precautions to ensure a healthy and stress-free trip. Start by researching the current health guidelines and travel advisories in place. Stay updated on vaccination requirements and health protocols specific to Kyoto and Japan.

Ensure you have comprehensive travel insurance that covers medical emergencies and unexpected health-related situations. Consult your healthcare provider to discuss any vaccinations or health precautions recommended for travelers to Japan.

Staying Healthy on the Plane

Long flights can take a toll on your health, so it's essential to take precautions during your journey. Stay hydrated by drinking plenty of water, avoid excessive alcohol consumption, and move around the cabin periodically to prevent deep vein thrombosis.

Consider wearing compression socks, practicing simple stretches, and getting adequate rest during the flight. These measures will help you arrive in Kyoto feeling refreshed and ready to explore.

Accommodation Health Considerations

Choose accommodations that prioritize cleanliness and hygiene. Research hotels, hostels, or guesthouses that have implemented robust sanitation practices. Ensure that your chosen lodging follows local health guidelines and protocols.

Pack essential hygiene items, including hand sanitizer, disinfectant wipes, and any personal protective equipment you deem necessary. Take the time to sanitize high-touch surfaces in your accommodation upon arrival for an added layer of precaution.

Eating and Drinking Safely

Kyoto boasts a diverse and delectable culinary scene, but it's essential to prioritize food safety. Opt for restaurants and street vendors with good hygiene practices. Ensure that your food is thoroughly cooked, especially when trying local delicacies.

Stay hydrated with bottled or purified water and be cautious with consuming raw or undercooked foods. If you have dietary restrictions or allergies, communicate them clearly to restaurant staff to avoid any health issues.

Exploring Kyoto: Outdoor Health Precautions

Kyoto's charm lies in its temples, gardens, and outdoor attractions. While exploring, be mindful of the weather conditions. Dress appropriately, wear sunscreen, and stay hydrated, especially during the warmer months.

Follow local health guidelines regarding mask-wearing and social distancing, and be respectful of cultural norms. If you plan to engage in physical activities such as hiking, ensure you are in good health and adequately prepared with suitable gear.

Medical Services and Emergency Contacts

Familiarize yourself with local medical services and emergency contacts in Kyoto. Know the location of the nearest hospitals, clinics, and pharmacies. Keep essential medical information and contacts readily accessible, and consider utilizing translation apps to overcome language barriers if necessary.

A trip to Kyoto can be an enriching experience when health precautions are prioritized. By taking proactive measures before and during your visit, you can ensure a safe and enjoyable exploration of this culturally rich city. Remember to stay informed, maintain good hygiene practices, and be mindful of your health throughout your journey in Kyoto.

Emergency contact numbers

Kyoto, with its rich history, cultural heritage, and vibrant atmosphere, attracts millions of visitors every year. While exploring this enchanting city, it's crucial to be prepared for any unforeseen circumstances by having access to emergency contact numbers. This aims to provide you with essential information about emergency services in Kyoto, ensuring your safety and well-being during your visit.

Police Services:

In case of emergencies requiring police assistance, Kyoto has a dedicated police force ready to respond promptly. The general emergency police line is 110, which you can dial from any phone, including payphones. This number connects you to the Kyoto Prefectural Police, who can assist with a wide range of emergencies, including theft, accidents, and other criminal activities.

Additionally, each ward in Kyoto has its own police station. If you need assistance that is not of an immediate emergency nature, you can find the contact information for the specific police station in your area. They can provide information, assistance, and support for non-urgent matters.

Fire and Ambulance Services:

Kyoto has a well-established emergency response system for fires, accidents, and medical emergencies. To request fire or ambulance services, dial 119. This number connects you to the Kyoto City Fire Department, where trained professionals are ready to respond to any emergency, including fires, accidents, and medical situations.

When calling 119, it's crucial to provide clear information about the nature of the emergency, your location, and any other relevant details. The operators are trained to dispatch the appropriate emergency services based on the information you provide.

Medical Emergencies:

Kyoto boasts a robust healthcare system, with numerous hospitals and clinics throughout the city. In the event of a medical emergency, calling for an ambulance (119) is the quickest way to receive assistance. The paramedics will transport you to the nearest hospital equipped to handle your specific medical needs.

It's also helpful to be aware of the location and contact information of the nearest hospitals and clinics in your area. This information can be obtained from your accommodation or the local tourist information centers. Keep in mind that not all medical facilities may have English-speaking staff, so it's advisable to have a translation app or a local friend who can assist in case of language barriers.

Embassies and Consulates:

While not directly emergency services, knowing the contact information for your country's embassy or consulate is essential for handling certain situations. They can assist with issues such as lost passports, legal matters, and other non-medical emergencies. Be sure to have this information readily available, and if possible, register with your embassy online before your trip.

Local Support Services:

Kyoto offers various local support services that can assist with non-emergency situations. For instance, if you find yourself lost or in need of general information, the Kyoto Tourist Information Centers located throughout the city can provide guidance. Additionally, there are multilingual hotlines and services designed to assist tourists with a wide range of inquiries.

While Kyoto is generally a safe destination, unforeseen emergencies can happen. Being aware of the emergency contact numbers and available services is a crucial aspect of responsible travel. Take the time to familiarize yourself with this information before your trip, and share it with your travel companions. By staying informed and prepared, you can ensure a safer and more enjoyable experience in this captivating city. Remember, it's always better to be proactive and have the necessary information at hand in case of any unexpected situations.

CONCLUSION

In conclusion, this guide stands as an indispensable companion for anyone seeking to explore the rich tapestry of Kyoto's cultural heritage, natural beauty, and timeless traditions. Throughout its pages, the guide unfolds a narrative that goes beyond the conventional boundaries of travel literature, inviting readers into the heart of Kyoto's enchanting world.

The allure of Kyoto lies not only in its picturesque landscapes but also in the deep-rooted traditions that have stood the test of time. This guide meticulously unravels the layers of Kyoto's history, offering readers a profound understanding of the city's cultural significance. From the iconic Fushimi Inari Shrine with its vermillion torii gates to the tranquility of the Kinkaku-ji, each page of the guide is a gateway to a new discovery, a testament to the author's commitment to capturing the essence of Kyoto.

One of the guide's notable strengths is its ability to cater to diverse interests and preferences. Whether you are a history buff eager to explore ancient temples, a nature enthusiast yearning for the tranquility of bamboo groves, or a food lover ready to embark on a culinary journey through Kyoto's vibrant markets, this guide has something for everyone. It seamlessly weaves together practical travel information with insightful anecdotes, ensuring that every reader can tailor their Kyoto experience to suit their individual tastes.

Beyond being a mere logistical handbook, the guide takes on the role of a cultural ambassador, encouraging readers to immerse themselves in the local way of life. The guide fosters an appreciation for the delicate art of the tea ceremony, the elegance of traditional kimonos, and the meticulous craftsmanship of Kyoto's artisans. It is not just a book but a gateway to an immersive experience, beckoning readers to step into Kyoto's world with open hearts and inquisitive minds.

Moreover, the guide's user-friendly format and detailed maps provide a sense of reassurance to travelers navigating the labyrinthine streets of Kyoto. It goes beyond the standard tourist recommendations, offering insider tips that empower readers to venture off the beaten path and uncover hidden gems. In doing so, the guide transforms a visit to Kyoto into a personal odyssey, a journey of self-discovery and cultural appreciation.

In essence, this guide transcends the boundaries of a typical travel companion. It is a portal to a city where tradition and modernity coalesce, where every street corner reveals a story, and where the spirit of Kyoto unfolds like a delicate cherry blossom in spring. For anyone embarking on a journey to this timeless city, this guide is not just a book; it is an invaluable companion that ensures every step taken in Kyoto is a step into the extraordinary. So, let the pages of the guide be your compass, guiding you through the wonders of Kyoto and leaving you with memories that linger long after the journey has ended.

Made in the USA
Las Vegas, NV
18 March 2024

87403887R00085